# DISCOVERING
# LONDON RAILWAY
# STATIONS

Oliver Green

D0808551

Published in association with
London Transport Museum

SHIRE PUBLICATIONS

Published in Great Britain in 2010 by Shire Publications Ltd, Midland House, West Way, Botley, Oxford OX2 0PH, United Kingdom.

44-02 23rd Street, Suite 219, Long Island City, NY 11101, USA.

E-mail: shire@shirebooks.co.uk    www.shirebooks.co.uk

A CIP catalogue record for this book is available from the British Library.

Shire Discovering no. 303.    ISBN-13: 978 0 74780 806 0

Oliver Green has asserted his right under the Copyright, Designs and Patents Act, 1988, to be identified as the author of this book.

Designed by Tony Truscott Designs and typeset in Garamond.

Printed in China through Worldprint Ltd.

10 11 12 13 14    10 9 8 7 6 5 4 3 2 1

COVER: *Going North? St. Pancras*, a Midland Railway poster by Fred Taylor, 1910.

ACKNOWLEDGEMENTS

The author is grateful to the following who have provided images and permission for reproduction on these pages: Getty Images, pages 5, 15, 50, 54, 64, 91, and 93; London Transport Museum/Transport for London, pages 7, 8, 10, 23, 24, 26 (bottom), 30, 31, 40, 51, 58, 60, 66, 70, 71, 72, 73, 80, 82, 84, 90, 97, 98, 100, and 101; National Railway Museum/Science & Society Picture Library, cover and pages 28, 36, 39, 48, 52, 77, 85, and 88; Network Rail, pages 9, 53, 75, and 78. All other photographs were taken by Oliver Green, and the postcard view on page 35 is from his own collection.

# CONTENTS

# INTRODUCTION

LONDON has more main line railway stations than any other city in the world. Its earliest terminals opened in the late 1830s when lines between the capital and the regions were built in the first railway boom. The original station at London Bridge, the capital's first passenger terminus, opened in December 1836, six months before Queen Victoria came to the throne. The last main line to London, terminating at Marylebone, opened in March 1899, two years before the elderly queen died.

The development of a railway network transformed Great Britain in the nineteenth century. Passenger journeys that had taken days by road were reduced to hours by rail. Heavy and bulky goods that in 1820 could be transported only by ship and canal barge could be distributed anywhere by train forty or fifty years later. A railway system soon covered the whole of Britain, making the most remote areas accessible and opening up new markets for agricultural and industrial products.

Most of the early steam railways were built in the industrial North, where at first they carried coal rather than people. The Stockton & Darlington was the first to carry passengers in 1825, but its main purpose and business was shifting coal. Five years later, the Liverpool & Manchester Railway was the first to be built as an inter-city passenger route. Its success soon led to plans to construct main lines to London.

Every proposal to build a railway had to be approved by Parliament. Some schemes were turned down or failed to raise the substantial capital investment required for construction. All of them were privately funded, and there was very little attempt by the government to regulate the market or plan an integrated network, either for London or for the rest of the country. Growth was rapid but chaotic, with a good deal of duplication as a result of fierce competition between rival companies.

By 1901 London's railway infrastructure, built up throughout Victoria's long reign, was enormous. Stations, depots, yards, tracks, bridges and other railway facilities such as hotels and stables covered huge areas of the capital. The world's largest city had grown to depend on its railway links to function. London's food and coal supplies were brought in by train. Its manufactured and imported goods were distributed by rail. National newspapers and the Royal Mail went by train. Thousands of Londoners were employed by the railways and many more, such as cab drivers and hotel staff, depended on them for much of their work.

The main line stations became the gateways to London. Anyone travelling to or from the metropolis on business or pleasure took the train and passed through one of the great railway terminals. This included a growing army of season-ticket holders travelling daily to work in the City or Westminster, and back to their homes in London's spreading suburbs or beyond. The lifestyle of the London commuter still depends heavily on this overground passenger rail

Waterloo, London's largest and busiest station. This photograph was taken in November 2007, on the last day that Eurostar services operated from Waterloo International (in the foreground) before transferring to St Pancras.

network today. More than half the people who now work in central and inner London use the national rail system for their daily journey. By the beginning of the twentieth century this network had grown almost to its maximum extent in Greater London.

Statistics compiled for the Royal Commission on London Traffic in 1903 showed nearly 300 million annual passenger journeys being made through the capital's rail terminals. A century later, the total was over 400 million and rising, though London's once-massive rail freight and parcels traffic had almost disappeared. The huge former goods yards are still being redeveloped for housing, retail, leisure and other uses, notably north of King's Cross, and at Stratford, where the main 2012 Olympics site and the giant Westfield shopping complex are both on former railway lands.

The main Victorian railway terminals nearly all still exist, though some have been resited and others partly or completely rebuilt. Only two of the City terminals, Broad Street and Holborn Viaduct, have been closed, demolished and wiped off the map. There was no original grand plan to co-ordinate their siting or construction, which was undertaken by more than a dozen separate railway companies in the nineteenth century. These independently run organisations rarely worked together unless made to do so, such as the forced grouping into just four big private companies imposed by the government in 1923. The London terminals were designed in the nineteenth century as statements of each railway's ambition and individuality. They were never rationalised in the twentieth century despite nationalisation in 1948 and various attempts since the 1960s to modernise them.

The concept of the *Hauptbahnhof*, or grand central station, where nearly all train services for a big urban centre meet under one roof, has been adopted in many European cities such as Amsterdam, Milan and most recently Berlin. It was also used in big American cities, including New York, Chicago and Washington, although today the much-reduced passenger rail services of the United States are very limited by European standards. Concentration in a single station would not have suited a vast metropolis like London, the ultimate railway town. On the Continent, Paris remains the leading rail city, with services to and from six principal terminals. But London still wins hands down, with thirteen busy terminal stations.

It is likely that demand for rail travel in London will continue to grow rather than diminish. As a result, there are various development schemes scheduled or under way to improve capacity but no plans to close any of the stations described here. London's largely Victorian passenger railway infrastructure will be further adapted but not reduced to meet the needs of the twenty-first century. A tour of the terminals is a fascinating trip through more than 170 years of change and growth, with surviving features visible from nearly every period.

This book is a guide to London's main rail terminals, and designed to be used on a circular tour of central London, starting at Paddington in the north-west and moving clockwise. Most of the stations described are served by, or close to, London Underground's Circle line, which was originally planned to link the main line terminals. It is the easiest way to travel on the circuit, although cycling is cheaper and probably quicker. Line changes or short walks are needed to get to Marylebone, Fenchurch Street, London Bridge and Waterloo.

*Waterloo Station Centenary* by Helen McKie, 1947, the last poster issued by the Southern Railway before nationalisation.

Postcard view of Broad Street station, 1907. The terminus was closed and demolished in 1986.

Underground and Docklands Light Railway stations in central London with terminal platforms, such as Baker Street, Bank and Moorgate, have been excluded, as well as major through stations and interchange points such as Clapham Junction, Farringdon, City Thameslink and Stratford, although these can be as busy as some of the terminals.

## Station opening dates

Existing terminals are shown in capitals, closed stations in italics, with the railway company responsible for the first station on each site and the original opening date. They are listed in date order.

LONDON BRIDGE: London & Greenwich Railway, 14 December 1836.
EUSTON: London & Birmingham Railway, 20 July 1837.
*Nine Elms* (*Vauxhall*): London & Southampton Railway, 21 May 1838.
*Paddington 1*: Great Western Railway, 4 June 1838.
*Shoreditch*: Eastern Counties Railway, 1 July 1840.
*Minories*: London & Blackwall Railway, 6 July 1840.

FENCHURCH STREET: London & Blackwall Railway, 2 August 1841.

*Bricklayers Arms*: South Eastern Railway, 1 May 1844.

WATERLOO: London & South Western Railway, 11 July 1848.

*Maiden Lane*: Great Northern Railway, 7 August 1850.

KING'S CROSS: Great Northern Railway, 14 October 1852.

PADDINGTON: Great Western Railway, 16 January 1854.

*Pimlico*: West End of London & Crystal Palace Railway, 29 March 1858.

VICTORIA: London, Brighton & South Coast Railway, 1 October 1860.

CHARING CROSS: South Eastern Railway, 11 January 1864.

*Blackfriars (Bridge)*: London, Chatham & Dover Railway, 1 June 1864.

*Ludgate Hill*: London, Chatham & Dover Railway, 1 June 1865.

*Broad Street*: North London Railway, 1 November 1865.

CANNON STREET: South Eastern Railway, 1 September 1866.

ST PANCRAS: Midland Railway, 1 October 1868.

LIVERPOOL STREET: Great Eastern Railway, 2 February 1874.

*Holborn Viaduct*: London, Chatham & Dover Railway, 2 March 1874.

BLACKFRIARS (originally St Paul's): London, Chatham & Dover Railway, 10 May 1886.

MARYLEBONE: Great Central Railway, 15 March 1899.

The new Blackfriars station will extend right across the railway bridge to the south bank of the Thames, close to Tate Modern.

# UNDERGROUND

# PADDINGTON

## NEW STATION

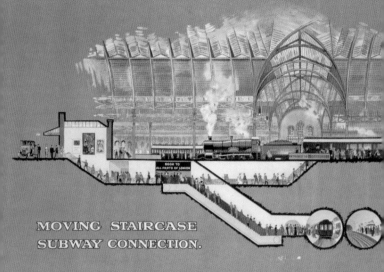

MOVING STAIRCASE
SUBWAY CONNECTION.

# OPENS
# DECEMBER 1ST.

# LINKS THE G.W.R.
# WITH ALL PARTS OF
# LONDON.

# PADDINGTON

PADDINGTON is the best-preserved of London's Victorian terminals. To step off a train under Isambard Kingdom Brunel's great triple-span iron and glass roof is one of the most dramatic ways to arrive in London. The station probably looks better today, cleaned and renovated, than at any time since the 1860s, and one's arrival is a moment to savour.

What we see now is not the original London terminus of the Great Western Railway (GWR). The line was built to link London with Bristol, and later the West Country, West Midlands and South Wales. In 1835, when construction work began on the section of line just west of London near Ealing, the final site of the terminus had not been chosen. Brunel, the GWR's Chief Engineer, had discussions with Robert Stephenson, whose London & Birmingham Railway (L&BR) was approaching from the north-west, about creating a dual terminus for the two lines at Euston. However, no agreement could be reached and the L&BR occupied the Euston site alone, opening the capital's first inter-city main line terminus there in 1837.

Brunel already favoured Paddington, probably because the site was adjacent to the basin of the Grand Junction Canal, which had opened there in 1801, followed by the Regent's Canal in 1820. The potential for transhipment of goods on to the canals was an important consideration for the early railways. The two canals had

Opposite: London Underground poster showing the new Bakerloo Tube station at Paddington, 1913.

already encouraged the rapid growth of Paddington from a village into the developed western edge of London. George Shillibeer introduced London's first omnibus service between Paddington and the Bank of England in 1829.

Brunel had persuaded the GWR directors to build a broad-gauge railway, with the rails 7 feet 0¼ inch apart. The London & Birmingham used the 4 foot 8½ inch gauge already standard in the rest of the country. The broad gauge would have made a joint terminus more complicated, though not impossible. Brunel got his way with his more expensive broad gauge to Paddington, though it was not to last. In 1861, just two years after his death, the GWR introduced mixed-gauge tracks to London, and in 1892 the last broad-gauge express left Paddington for Plymouth.

Because of the high cost of the land purchased for the Paddington route and site, the GWR could only afford to build a rather small wooden passenger terminus for the opening of the line in 1838. It stood just north of the current station, on the site now occupied by the new high-rise office development between the railway and the canal basin. The original station entrance was under the arches of the first Bishop's Road Bridge, which was built right across the site. The low-level cutting alongside Eastbourne Terrace, where the present station stands, was originally used for a goods shed. Later, the areas used for the permanent passenger station and a large goods depot were effectively swapped over.

The first Paddington has been described as a makeshift affair. Architecturally, it was no match for Euston, and passenger facilities were very basic. Services to Maidenhead started in June 1838, extending to Reading in 1840 and through to Bristol in 1841. On 13 June 1842 Queen Victoria herself travelled by train for the first time, between Slough and Paddington, and announced that she was 'quite charmed' with the experience. The Royal Family became regular rail users when travelling between London and Windsor Castle.

As the GWR's traffic grew rapidly in the 1840s, the inadequacies of its cramped temporary terminus at the London end of the line became more obvious. Eventually, in 1850, Brunel was asked to design a much larger new station on the present Paddington site.

Building technology had moved on and Brunel's second station was clearly influenced by Joseph Paxton's iron and glass Crystal Palace, which had won the competition to house the 1851 Great Exhibition in Hyde Park. Brunel was on the Exhibition committee and had seen his own proposal beaten by Paxton's giant glasshouse, but he seemed quite willing to learn from this revolutionary design.

In January 1851 he wrote to the architect Matthew Digby Wyatt, who was secretary of the Exhibition committee: 'I am going to design, in a great hurry … a Station after my own fancy … It is at Paddington, in a cutting, and admitting of no exterior, all interior and all roofed in.' Brunel asked Wyatt to act as his assistant on the decorative details and approached the engineering contractors Fox Henderson, who were responsible for assembling the Crystal Palace, to build the new station. In December 1851 the GWR board engaged another architect, Philip Charles Hardwick, who had just completed the Great Hall at Euston, to design a large hotel in front of the station on Praed Street.

The grand new Paddington station and Great Western Royal Hotel were completed and opened in 1854. Brunel's station included a suite of royal waiting rooms alongside Platform 1, still in use today as the first-class lounge. Work on the outlying new facilities around the old station site, which included a huge goods depot, engine, carriage and wagon sheds, continued until 1857. Altogether, these improvements at Paddington cost the GWR nearly £700,000.

Brunel died in 1859, aged only fifty-three, worn out by the stress of his final engineering project, the construction of the *Great Eastern*, then the largest ship ever built. Daniel Gooch, the GWR's locomotive engineer, wrote of his friend and colleague: 'the commercial world thought him extravagant, but although he was so, great things are not done by those who sit down and count the cost of every thought and act.' Brunel rarely relaxed, which makes John Doubleday's 1982 statue of the great engineer, now positioned in the taxi rank exit at Paddington, seem a little inappropriate. Brunel sits surveying the interior of his great trainshed, an unlikely pose for such a workaholic, but he is clutching his famous stovepipe hat in his left hand, ready to rush off to another site inspection.

Brunel's 1854 trainshed 150 years after completion, still an elegant and practical station interior.

Brunel's Paddington station is a light and elegant design, but also an extremely sound and functional piece of engineering, which has served its purpose for more than 150 years. The track and platform layout have been changed considerably over the years, but all this has been possible with Brunel's cast-iron and glass trainshed as the core of the station. Wyatt's main contributions as architectural collaborator were the attractive metal tracery on the end screens of the shed, the decorative motifs on the columns, and the two sets of oriel windows on the first floor of the office building overlooking Platform 1.

The Moorish design style at Paddington shows the influence of Owen Jones, who had been Superintendent of Works for the Great Exhibition. Wyatt consulted him over the decoration at Paddington just as Jones was preparing his monumental full-colour pattern book of decorative motifs, the *Grammar of Ornament*, published in 1856. All these superb original features remain and were enhanced with a new lighting scheme as part of the major station refurbishment carried out in the 1990s.

Paddington is the subject of one of the best-known Victorian paintings, William Powell Frith's *The Railway Station*, completed in 1862. Frith used Paddington as the setting for an artfully contrived panorama of Victorian society, featuring more than sixty characters on the station platform. Rather as Brunel employed Wyatt as his assistant, Frith got another artist, William Scott Morton, to help him

The Wyatt end screen of the trainshed pictured in 1933.

paint inanimate details like the station architecture and a train. The result is a lively picture in which even the locomotive, one of Gooch's broad-gauge 'Iron Duke' Class engines, is shown in accurate detail. The very large oil painting has been on display in London University's Royal Holloway College at Egham since the 1880s.

In January 1863 the world's first underground railway, the Metropolitan, opened between Paddington and Farringdon, giving the Great Western access by rail to the City of London. There was a junction with the GWR main line just outside Paddington, and a separate station for the Metropolitan called Bishop's Road. This soon became a through station when services began in 1864 over a new extension line westwards to a terminus at Hammersmith. Originally there was no connection for passengers between the Hammersmith & City Line station and the main Paddington terminus, but a footbridge link was added in 1870. Rebuilding to create a suburban section as part of the main Paddington station took place in the 1930s, when the name 'Bishop's Road' disappeared.

A second underground station at Paddington, originally called Praed Street, was opened over the road from the Great Western Royal Hotel in 1868 when a branch of the Metropolitan was opened running southwards to Kensington. This is now the District and Circle Lines station, which was partly rebuilt in 1914 with a new booking hall at street level, but it still retains its original 1860s platform walls and part of the overall roof. Underground services through both Bishop's Road and Praed Street stations were electrified in 1905.

At the start of the twentieth century, when Paddington was used as a staging point for Queen Victoria's funeral procession to Windsor in 1901, the GWR's traffic was outgrowing Brunel's trainshed. In the 1850s only twenty

The GWR coat of arms over the Praed Street entrance to Paddington.

trains a day left Paddington. By 1907 it was three hundred every twenty-four hours. Since 1903 the great three-faced clock over Platform 1, which was designed and made by Kays of Worcester, has watched over every departure. It was mechanically driven until 1929, when it was converted to electric operation, controlled from the station-master's office.

A new fourth roof span, on steel rather than cast-iron supports, was added to Brunel's three-arched trainshed in 1913–15 to provide additional covered platform space. This was mainly to accommodate the growth of suburban services, although, in contrast to Liverpool Street and London Bridge, Paddington was still dominated by

The GWR war memorial on Platform 1 at Paddington.

long-distance trains. The GWR never considered itself a suburban railway. From December 1913 Paddington gained a direct Tube connection with the West End, when an extension to the Bakerloo Line opened, with escalators to the new deep-level platforms directly below the main line station.

More than 2,500 GWR employees were killed in the First World War, and a memorial to them was commissioned for Paddington by the railway company. It is prominently sited halfway along Platform 1 and was dedicated on Armistice Day 1922. The larger than lifesize bronze figure of a British infantryman reading a letter from home is by Charles Sergeant Jagger. It is one of the finest war memorials in London, and poppy wreaths are still placed there every November.

Despite the further expansion and rebuilding in the early twentieth century of the Paddington goods depot on the site of the original terminus, the main station continued to handle extensive non-passenger traffic. Most of the GWR's market traffic came through

Paddington. In the 1920s this included 50 to 200 tons a day of flowers, fish, fruit, meat and vegetables, and about 5,500 milk churns from the West Country, together with more than 200 tons of newspapers going out of London to the west every night. Even more important was the huge business served by the parcels and mail departments at Paddington. At Christmas 1936, when both sections would have been working at their peak, the GWR proudly reported having shifted nearly eighty thousand parcel-post bags in twenty-eight special train loads.

In the early 1930s there was an attempt to improve Paddington's rather primitive and antiquated passenger facilities, prompted by the approaching centenary of the GWR in 1935. The area between the rear of the hotel and the station platforms, which had been used as a loading area for vehicles, was turned into a proper passenger concourse. This space has always been called the Lawn at Paddington, although there has not been a blade of grass there since construction of the present station began. It may have been the site of the stationmaster's garden when the temporary terminus was opened in 1838, and for some reason the name has stuck.

One of Wyatt's oriel windows overlooking the platforms at Paddington.

The Victorian hotel was given a modish 1930s refurbishment inside and out, with a new lounge overlooking the Lawn. A large modern office block in matching Art Deco style was built alongside the station entrance ramp from Praed Street, designed by the Great Western's architect, P. A. Culverhouse. Look up as you enter or leave the station this way to see 'GWR PADDINGTON' still proclaimed in giant raised letters at the top of the building, illuminated at night by stylish shell-shaped 1930s uplighters.

Paddington was badly damaged during the Second World War, with direct hits on the station and the Eastbourne Terrace buildings, which had to be partly demolished. The station was a departure point for hundreds of children evacuated from London to the countryside on the outbreak of war in September 1939. Each child had a small suitcase and a label tied to his or her coat. This was part of the inspiration for the popular children's character Paddington Bear, created by the author Michael Bond in the 1950s. Named after the station where he was found in the original story, Paddington was a stowaway from 'darkest Peru'. He now has a permanent place on the Lawn as a bronze sculpture, complete with suitcase, based on the original book illustrations by Peggy Fortnum. A specially designed stall on the concourse sells all the Paddington Bear books and branded merchandise.

The GWR became the Western Region of British Railways on nationalisation in 1948, but there was little money available to repair war damage, and none to modernise the station. Steam trains were replaced by diesels between 1959 and 1965, and in the 1970s diesel High Speed Trains (HSTs) were introduced. Modernised and refurbished HSTs are still used on most long-distance services from Paddington, now run by First Great Western. Plans to electrify Brunel's main line have been announced but will take many years to complete.

The bronze statue of Paddington Bear on the Lawn.

In the 1990s a major refurbishment of the station was carried out. This included the creation of an open retail and café area on the Lawn, with a glazed screen to Brunel's trainshed; a very effective reworking by Nicholas Grimshaw & Partners that has improved the station's facilities but also enhanced its historic features.

The first electric trains arrived at Paddington in 1998 with the inauguration of the Heathrow Express service, which provides a direct train to the airport every fifteen minutes, with a journey time of fifteen minutes. It is easily the fastest way to get to Heathrow, but it is said to be the most expensive rail journey in Europe. There are airport check-in facilities on the remodelled concourse.

The Paddington goods depot site north of the station was completely redeveloped in the first decade of the twenty-first century with high-rise offices. Network Rail, which now runs the station, had plans to demolish the fourth roof span and build a raft over the tracks to create even more commercial office space above the suburban platforms. This scheme has now been abandoned, and the fourth span is being renovated and restored.

The next major scheduled development at Paddington is Crossrail. This will be a new railway under central London linking Heathrow and the main line to the west with the east of the city. There will be direct interchange with the Underground at key points in the West End, City and at Canary Wharf. Crossrail services will leave the Great Western main line just outside Paddington and run eastwards in tunnel from Royal Oak, surfacing again on the other side of London outside Liverpool Street, and in Docklands.

The Crossrail platforms at Paddington will be on the Eastbourne Terrace axis of the station alongside Brunel's trainshed. Natural light will be brought down to the underground platforms in a great slit trench with a glazed roof. As a combined architectural and engineering concept on a grand scale, this project is firmly in the Brunel tradition. Unfortunately, Crossrail has been subject to funding and planning problems since the early 1990s. Construction work began in 2009, and completion and opening of the new line is scheduled for 2017.

# MARYLEBONE

**M**ARYLEBONE was built as the terminus of the last main line into London, which brought the Great Central Railway to the capital. The station was opened on 15 March 1899. It was never a great success and in the early 1980s a plan to convert the rail line into a coach route with Marylebone as a bus station was being given serious consideration. Fortunately this idea was abandoned and a major programme of investment began which has dramatically reversed the station's fortunes. Marylebone's prospects for the future now look better than at any time in the twentieth century.

The driving force behind the original project was Sir Edward Watkin, one of the most energetic and far-sighted of the Victorian railway barons. Watkin was chairman of the Manchester, Sheffield & Lincolnshire Railway (MSLR) and had grandiose plans to extend its main line through the Midlands to London. The MSLR's change of name in 1897 to the Great Central Railway (GCR) confirmed the scale of his ambition. Watkin was already chairman of the Metropolitan and South Eastern Railways, and of a company planning to build a Channel tunnel. His ultimate aim was to link all these projects together and create a rail route from Manchester to Paris.

The GCR's approach to London was over the Metropolitan Railway's main line from Buckinghamshire, and then on new parallel tracks from Harrow through the north-west suburbs to Finchley Road. From here, where the Met dives underground to Baker Street, a new line was needed to take the GCR another 2 miles through St John's Wood, mainly in tunnel, to Marylebone. A large site was cleared for a goods and coal depot beside the Regent's Canal and the passenger terminus was planned just beyond this point, to be fronted by a grand hotel on the Marylebone Road.

Preparations for the final approach to Marylebone were both costly and controversial. The GCR built six large tenement blocks just off St John's Wood Road, in a new estate named Wharncliffe Gardens, to rehouse about three thousand of nearly 4,500 people whose homes had to be demolished. The railway goods yard included a massive five-storey warehouse, which took three years to build. This was later destroyed in a bombing raid in 1941. Both the GCR housing and the entire Marylebone goods yard site were redeveloped in the 1960s by the Greater London Council to create the Lisson Green Estate.

There was a much bigger fuss about the need to build the railway under Lord's, home of the Marylebone Cricket Club (MCC). When word got out in 1890 of the threat to the sacred turf, *Punch* magazine published a cartoon showing the eminent batsman

Described by John Betjeman as resembling a 'branch public library', modest Marylebone in 2010.

W. G. Grace leading his cricket team out to meet the enemy: Watkin and the GCR. To placate the MCC, the GCR had to guarantee that all necessary work would be carried out between the end of one cricketing season and the start of the next. Work eventually began at Lord's on 1 September 1896. The turf was carefully removed, the tunnels excavated and built at record speed, and the reinstated pitch was handed back to the MCC just eight months later, on 8 May 1897. Not one day's cricket had been lost and the club had gained nearly 2 acres of land as part of the deal.

Because of the high expense of getting its line to Marylebone, the GCR economised on its passenger terminus. The station buildings were designed not by an architect but by one of the engineering staff, H. W. Braddock. It is a modest construction in red brick, hidden from the Marylebone Road by the enormous bulk of the Great Central Hotel. As the railway historian Alan Jackson aptly commented, 'the result would have been creditable as council offices for a minor provincial town, but was hardly worthy as the London terminus of a railway that aspired to be in the first rank.' Sir John Betjeman thought Marylebone looked like a branch public library.

Marylebone forecourt with the station on the left and Great Central Hotel on the right, 1923. The view is almost unchanged today (see opposite).

An elegant iron and glass canopy over the entrance yard connects the station with the Great Central Hotel. As the railway had run out of money, the hotel was financed as a separate enterprise by Sir John Blundell Maple and lavishly fitted out with a marble staircase and a series of period rooms by his family furnishing company. The architect was Colonel Robert William Edis, who spared no expense on the Renaissance exterior and the grand dining and reception rooms within. The nine-storey hotel was built round a great glazed central courtyard, and there was even a cycle track on the roof for energetic guests.

Neither the station nor the hotel prospered. Sir Edward Watkin had stepped down as chairman of the GCR following a debilitating stroke before his new terminus was completed. When Marylebone was formally opened in March 1899 by C. T. Ritchie, President of the Board of Trade, the ailing Watkin attended the ceremony and luncheon for seven hundred guests in a Bath chair. He died two years later.

The Great Central Hotel, one of Sir John Blundell Maple's Frederick Hotels group, opened four months after the station, on 1 July. It is unlikely that the seven hundred bedrooms were ever fully booked, and traffic through the station could not have filled them.

Postcard view of Marylebone station concourse, 1907.

At this time there were just eleven trains a day scheduled each way in and out of Marylebone, seven of them expresses to and from Manchester. The trains were luxurious but slow, and the GCR's station porters were often said to outnumber the passengers. Maple died in 1903 and did not live to see his grand hotel make a profit.

The GCR never became a serious challenger to the other main line companies with long-distance trains, but it did develop successful outer suburban services, which became the mainstay of Marylebone. These were run in agreement with the Metropolitan Railway over the joint line to Aylesbury and with the GWR over its newly opened route to High Wycombe from 1906. Both lines became popular with more affluent season-ticket holders, who travelled in from country towns such as Beaconsfield and Princes Risborough.

Marylebone became a convenient terminus for the West End when a Tube station on the extended Bakerloo Line was opened on the western side of the main line station in 1907. The original station name, Great Central, was dropped ten years later but has reappeared at the end of the Tube platforms alongside Marylebone, after being revealed during restoration of the wall tiles. The GCR's initials also survive, repeated in the decorative railings all along the main Marylebone station frontage opposite the hotel.

The Great Central Railway disappeared in 1923 when it was merged with a number of other companies to create the London & North Eastern Railway (LNER). In the following year traffic through Marylebone was boosted considerably by the British Empire Exhibition at Wembley, for which a ten-minute service of non-stop trains was introduced. Sporting events at Wembley Stadium, first used for the FA Cup Final in 1923, also brought large crowds through Marylebone, but these busy occasions only punctuated long periods of quiet.

When the railways were nationalised in 1948, the Great Central Hotel became the headquarters of the British Transport Commission, and later of British Railways (BR). The grand public rooms were stripped of their decorative features and the increasingly dowdy interior came to look like any other faceless government offices. Railway staff knew it as 'the Kremlin', or '222', from its postal address on Marylebone Road. BR eventually moved out in 1991 and the building was sold for reuse as a hotel. By now it was a listed building, and sensitive renovation has recreated a luxury hotel with much of the character it must have had when it first opened. It became the Landmark London Hotel in 1995.

Great Central Railway railings outside Marylebone station, 2010.

BR did attempt to revive main line services from Marylebone by introducing two named express trains in 1948, the 'Master Cutler' to Sheffield and the 'South Yorkshireman' to Bradford, but these were withdrawn in 1960. Diesel multiple units replaced steam on the suburban services from 1961, and five years later the old Great Central main line north of Aylesbury closed completely. By the end there were just three trains a day each way to Leicester and Nottingham and a single night service to and from

Subway entrance to the new Bakerloo Tube station at Marylebone, then called Great Central, 1907.

Manchester. These 'semi-fasts' were the last steam passenger trains in north London.

As the quietest of the London termini, Marylebone was ideal for filming. Scenes from two classic British movies of the 1960s were shot there: the Beatles' first film, *A Hard Day's Night*, in 1964, and *The Ipcress File*, a spy thriller with Michael Caine, in 1965. Marylebone continued to slumber through the 1970s, with declining services, until the threat of complete closure came in the early 1980s. But in 1986 Marylebone was reprieved and the newly created Network South East, the London regional sector of BR, announced an £85m 'total route modernisation project' for the station and line.

By the 1990s Marylebone was being completely refurbished with a new terrazzo-style passenger concourse and a reduced footprint for the platforms. The western span of the trainshed was removed, and the space used for commercial office development. By taking out the wide but unused cab road three platform faces could comfortably fit under the remaining double roofspan, with two new additional short platforms on the western side.

New 'Turbo' diesel units were introduced on what has come to be called the 'Chiltern Line' and all services were improved and upgraded. When British Rail was privatised in 1996, Chiltern Railways, the train operator that won the franchise, was in a strong position to develop the business. More station improvements and new trains followed as Marylebone celebrated its centenary. The conversion of the old booking hall into a Marks & Spencer 'Simply Food' shop, with a florist's next door on the concourse, was characteristic of the station's upmarket transformation.

Passenger numbers have grown rapidly, particularly for leisure rather than commuter travel, and customer care has been a high priority for Chiltern Railways. Long-distance services to Birmingham and the West Midlands have been introduced and there are plans to build a new rail link to reach Oxford. Chiltern has been the most innovative and entrepreneurial of the train-operating companies serving London, and the remarkable renaissance of Marylebone looks set to continue. Watkin would surely have approved.

# EUSTON

THE ORIGINAL STATION opened at Euston in July 1837 was London's first inter-city main line terminus, connecting the capital with Birmingham. London Bridge station had opened in the previous year, but trains from there ran initially only as far as Greenwich, a few miles down the river. The London & Birmingham Railway (L&BR), engineered by Robert Stephenson, was a much more ambitious and larger-scale project bringing the Midlands, and later the whole of the North-west, within easy reach of London for the first time. Euston is still London's main rail gateway to and from the North-west, but no trace of the old station survived the comprehensive redevelopment of the 1960s.

The railway authorised by Parliament in 1833 was to terminate at Camden Town, just north of the Regent's Canal. A year later, the L&BR board got permission for an extension, taking the line across the canal and just over a mile closer to central London. The station site, just north of the New Road at Euston Square, happened to be the very spot where in 1807 Richard Trevithick had first demonstrated a working steam locomotive, *Catch-me-who-can*, on a circular track. Trevithick's pioneering experiment led to nothing and it was nearly thirty years later that a full-scale passenger railway came to London.

The first section of line from Euston up to Camden was built on a severe gradient to bridge the canal. As early steam locomotives

Opposite: The Great Hall at Euston, built in 1849, shortly before it was demolished in 1962.

Euston soon after opening in 1837, when all trains were cable-hauled up Camden Bank and third-class carriages were open trucks.

were not very powerful, Stephenson decided to use cable haulage on the incline to Primrose Hill. A large stationary-engine house was built at Camden to drive a continuous cable that hauled trains up the hill. The carriages were detached from the cable at Camden, and steam locomotives took over for the journey north. The cable system was abandoned in 1844 but for many years each train required two steam engines for the climb out of Euston.

The originally proposed station site at Camden became a large goods depot with transfer facilities on to the canal, extensive horse stabling and an engine shed. The goods yard stables have survived to become part of Camden Lock market, and the goods locomotive roundhouse built in 1847, but used after 1865 as a warehouse for Gilbey's gin, has now found a new use as the Roundhouse theatre and performing arts centre. Although there are no longer any freight operations at Camden, at least some of the impressive infrastructure of the Victorian railway can still be appreciated, while just down the main line at Euston nothing remains.

In 1837 Euston station had just two wooden platforms, known respectively as the 'arrival stage' and the 'departure stage'. There were four tracks and a simple cast-iron and glass trainshed, with the station offices alongside the departure platform. On the other side of the offices a grand avenue was laid out from the New Road to the station, and a huge Doric arch, designed by Philip Hardwick, was built at the entrance in 1838. This 'grand but simple portico', as the railway directors described it, served no practical purpose but was an impressive symbol of the railway's new power. Its destruction in 1962 seemed to represent the end of the great age of steam and the eclipse of the railway as a major form of transport.

Hardwick's arch and screen would have formed a better centrepiece entrance to Euston if a matching terminus for the Great Western Railway had been built alongside to the west, as briefly proposed in 1835. After the GWR decided to go to Paddington instead, the L&BR's Euston site developed in an asymmetrical layout that soon compromised Hardwick's carefully balanced plan. In 1839 his two matching four-storey buildings, described as a hotel and a dormitory, were completed on either side of his classical screen. These pioneer railway hotels were very successful, but, when a large link block was added in the 1880s to create a single establishment, this central section completely obscured the dramatic approach to Hardwick's great arch from the Euston Road.

THE GRAND ENTRANCE TO THE METROPOLITAN STATION OF THE NORTH WESTERN RAILWAY
Drawn & Engraved for the British Gazetteer

Hardwick's Euston arch and screen, as built in 1838.

In 1846 the L&BR became part of a larger company, the London & North Western Railway (LNWR). Hardwick's son, also called Philip, was commissioned to extend the facilities at the LNWR's London terminus. He designed an enormous Great Hall as a combined passenger concourse and waiting-room, which was completed in 1849. Like his father's Doric arch, Hardwick's Great Hall was grand but not altogether practical. Samuel Sidney, writing only two years after it opened, complained that 'comfort has been sacrificed to magnificence'. The Great Hall was the largest single room in a new building complex that effectively split the station site and soon made it difficult to expand the tracks and platform space around it as traffic grew.

A scheme for the complete reconstruction of Euston was first considered in the 1890s, but the only improvements were piecemeal, such as the introduction of two new Tube connections in 1907, and electric trains on the suburban services to Watford in 1922. A year later, at the railway Grouping, the LNWR became part of the London Midland & Scottish Railway (LMS), biggest of the 'Big Four' companies. The LMS was soon proudly claiming to be 'the largest private enterprise in the British Empire' and almost inevitably got in competition with the London & North Eastern Railway (LNER) for faster express services between London and Scotland.

When the LNER introduced its streamlined 'Coronation' train on the 393-mile East Coast route in 1937, taking just six hours from King's Cross to Edinburgh, the LMS responded with the new 'Coronation Scot' service. This also used fashionably streamlined locomotives pulling specially designed sets of coaches, and covered the 399 miles up the heavier inclines of the West Coast route from Euston to Glasgow in 6½ hours. The same route was used by the fast overnight Scottish postal service, memorably publicised in the classic documentary *Night Mail*, made by the GPO Film Unit in 1936, which features W. H. Auden's poem of the same name and an innovative musical score by Benjamin Britten.

Celebrating Euston's centenary in 1938, the go-ahead LMS announced new plans to rebuild its main London station. An architect's perspective was released showing a giant building in monumental Art Deco style, which would combine station facilities, hotel, railway offices and even a heliport on the roof. War broke out before any work on this scheme had started. A smaller-scale version of what a 1930s-style Euston might have been like can still be seen at Leeds station, where the LMS architect W. H. Hamlyn designed the Queen's Hotel with a stylish new station entrance concourse alongside, all opened in 1938.

When British Railways (BR) took over in 1948 there was money available to patch up war damage and redecorate the Great Hall, but nothing more. Then in 1959 comprehensive rebuilding of Euston was on the agenda again as part of BR's full-scale modernisation and electrification of the main lines to Birmingham, Manchester and Liverpool. The plans included the destruction of both Euston's grand monuments, the Great Hall and the Doric arch. The loss of the Great Hall was probably inevitable as it stood in the way of a rational platform layout and could not have been moved. Dismantling the Euston Arch for re-erection elsewhere would have been possible but there was no official inclination to do so.

This became a major conservation battle, which was taken all the way to the Prime Minister, Harold Macmillan. He would not intervene, and the complete demolition of everything at old Euston was carried out with almost indecent haste in 1962. The new station, designed by BR London Midland Region architect R. L. Moorcroft, was opened by Queen Elizabeth II in 1968. It is far more functional than the previous motley collection of buildings on the site, but as architecture it is dull and uninspiring. There is no real sense of arrival, however you approach Euston. Taxis and cars are forced underground to deliver rail passengers, so most people come straight up into the main hall by escalator from a taxi or the Tube.

Try approaching Euston on foot at ground level and you will find no clear entrance route to the station. Walking across from the Euston Road, you have to negotiate a busy bus station and a bleak little plaza overshadowed by a poorly designed office development thrown up in front of the station in the 1970s. One of the office blocks houses Network Rail, the quasi-public sector company created in 2002 which is now responsible for managing Euston and

The statue of Robert Stephenson, engineer of the first inter-city main line, outside Euston in 2010.

all the other London terminals except Marylebone and Blackfriars. Outside its offices, the only visible link with the past is a Victorian statue of Robert Stephenson, who brought the railway here in the first place, relocated from his prominent original position at the Euston Road entrance.

Once inside the station, you find that the main hall is a large well-lit box with prominent destination boards but very little else. The model for this seems to have been an airport terminal, but without the lounge seating that departing air passengers would expect. At Euston there is very little seating, and it is clear that nobody is expected to wait on the concourse. The ambience is unwelcoming, the acres of space wasted. Shops, cafés and other passenger facilities are housed round the edge of the hall and are quite cramped and difficult to negotiate with luggage. Only the travel centre to one side works well as a space. The trains are tucked away out of sight beyond concrete ramps and barriers, and the low-roofed platforms give no sense of occasion when embarking on a journey north. All that you can see as you finally board your train are giant illuminated advertisements and rather pathetic plastic flowers decorating the grim concrete canopies.

The rebuilding of Euston in the 1960s was long overdue but it was done at the worst possible time. There was little interest then in retaining and refurbishing Victorian buildings, and the quality of the new architecture that was designed to replace them was often poor. Brutally comprehensive redevelopment was favoured over any attempt to combine and integrate old and new. If the Euston project had been planned thirty years later, the outcome would no doubt have been very different.

There is hope for Euston yet. The 'new' Euston is now nearly fifty years old itself and has seen very little refurbishment or remodelling in that time. Network Rail announced in 2007 that it wanted to redevelop the station again and was looking for commercial partners to achieve this. The third Euston is intended to become the London terminus for High Speed Two, a new main line railway to Birmingham and beyond, though this scheme has yet to be agreed and financed as a project.

A fascinating adjunct to this is a proposal to rebuild Hardwick's great arch in front of the redeveloped station and south of its original position. It would sit between the two small gate lodges built in 1870 on either side of the Euston Road entrance approach, which are the only remaining nineteenth-century buildings on the entire site. This is where Robert Stephenson's statue stood. Some 60 per cent of the original arch stonework has been rediscovered in a channel of the River Lea in east London, where it was used to plug a hole in the riverbed after being taken down in 1962. British Waterways salvaged the stones from the river in 2009 and the Euston Arch Trust was established to campaign for its re-erection.

In the words of Michael Palin, patron of the new trust, 'the restoration of Euston Arch would restore to London's oldest main line terminus some of the character and dignity of its great neighbours.' It would also give the station a distinctive and individual sense of place, which is completely lacking in the buildings of the 1960s and 1970s.

Postcard view of Euston with LNWR express trains from the North, *c.* 1908. This station was demolished in 1962.

# ST PANCRAS

'RAILWAY termini and hotels are to the nineteenth century what monasteries and cathedrals were to the thirteenth century. They are truly the only representative buildings we possess.' When this suggestion appeared in *Building News* in 1875, the writer would have been thinking of St Pancras in particular, where the railway terminus had recently opened and the station hotel in front of it was almost complete. St Pancras was already seen as a symbol of the age when it was brand-new. It was then, and remains to this day, the most spectacular of the great London railway stations.

Both the trainshed and the hotel at St Pancras, which were designed separately in different styles by an engineer and an architect, were built on the largest possible scale. They were grandiose statements of a railway company's ambition, but also a very practical and harmonious combination of elements. Over time, the hotel in particular became widely viewed as a high Victorian folly that no longer had a useful purpose, yet it could not be severed from the station. After decades of blight and uncertainty, both halves of this magnificent edifice have at last been restored and adapted to new use in the twenty-first century. St Pancras will not suffer the same ignominious fate as Euston.

St Pancras station was a late arrival in London, created because the Midland Railway (MR) wanted its own passenger terminus in

Opposite: The Midland Grand Hotel at St Pancras seen from the Euston Road, *c.* 1927, looming over King's Cross station on the far right.

the capital. In 1858 the company started running goods and coal trains from the industrial East Midlands to London over the Great Northern main line. As traffic grew, the company soon decided to build its own separate goods depot just north of King's Cross, and by 1863 had plans to reach this with its own new London Extension Line. The project grew from being primarily about freight access into a full-scale passenger main line, which of course required a suitably grand London terminus as well as a goods depot.

The Midland's London Extension Line, built in the 1860s, was designed by the MR's consulting engineer, William Henry Barlow, who also planned the layout and infrastructure of the large station and goods depot complex just north of the Euston Road. This was as close to central London as Parliament would permit the Midland to build. It still required massive property demolition on the route through Camden and in the areas known as Agar Town and Somers Town, which had grown up since the arrival of the first trunk line to nearby Euston thirty years earlier.

Seven streets of housing and a brand-new church were obliterated to make way for the new station. The railway company had to rebuild the church in Kentish Town, but there was no offer of compensation or rehousing for the thousands evicted from their homes. There was a greater outcry at the way the navvies began to cut through the old St Pancras burial ground without removing the remains of the dead with due care. In preparatory works to the site, human skeletons were scattered and mixed up as coffins were clumsily excavated and fell apart. The young Thomas Hardy, then training as an architect before he became a successful writer, was given the job of overseeing the gruesome work over several nights. He recalled the experience in a poem of 1882 called 'The Levelled Churchyard':

> We late-lamented, resting here
> Are mixed to human jam,
> And each to each exclaims in fear,
> 'I know not which I am!'…

Having bridged the canal, Barlow's main line approached the Euston Road at high level rather than coming down to street level on a steep gradient, like the route to Euston. The approach was also a contrast to the Great Northern, which runs into King's Cross through tunnels *under* the Regent's Canal. Barlow deliberately chose a high-level route and designed St Pancras with the passenger terminus platforms at first-floor level above a large ground-floor basement.

An enormous single-span cast-iron station roof 700 feet long, and reaching 100 feet above the tracks, was tied into the brick piers of the side walls. This gave a huge uninterrupted flexible space for the track and platform layout inside the station. The trainshed was the tallest and widest ever built. Barlow acknowledged the close collaboration of another leading Victorian engineer, Rowland Mason Ordish, who was responsible for the Albert Bridge in London, in the detailed design of the great roof.

In the basement cast-iron pillars and girders supported the station floor deck above and were divided into a grid based on the

Starting to erect Barlow's great trainshed at St Pancras, using a huge centring frame, which ran on rails across the platform deck, 1867.

Waiting for an arrival at St Pancras on the central cab road, *c.* 1910.

dimensions of the brewery warehouses in Burton upon Trent. As Barlow later put it himself, 'the length of a beer barrel became the unit of measure upon which all the arrangements of this floor were based.' The MR intended to run three special beer trains a day direct from the Midlands to London. At St Pancras the trains were to be split into individual wagon loads, which could be lowered by hydraulic lift to the vaults below the station, and moved around on tracks and turnplates using ropes. The beer barrels would then be unloaded on to horse-drawn drays for delivery to pubs. All this could be carried out within the footprint of the station without passengers and goods ever crossing each other's paths or competing for room, as happened at most busy railway terminals.

Barlow's station plan was a brilliant use of space and logistics, and the structure is a superb piece of engineering. St Pancras station was opened for both passenger and beer traffic in 1868, when the hotel, which was to form the frontage and entrance on Euston Road, had only just been started. Barlow had also built a separate goods station just across Midland Road to the west, on the site now occupied by the British Library. Underneath St Pancras station a curved tunnel took two tracks down to join the Metropolitan Railway. These 'Widened Lines', as they were known, ran in tunnel alongside the Met tracks to Moorgate, giving the Midland a link through to the City.

The Midland chose the architect for their Grand Hotel through holding a competition in 1865. The winning entry was by George Gilbert Scott, already the most famous Gothic Revival architect of the day. His imposing design in polychromatic brick, with a soaring spire and tower, was quite different to the first generation of railway hotels that preceded it. Above all, its appeal to the Midland directors was no doubt that Scott's building would completely overshadow the hotel and

The original 1868 booking office at St Pancras after restoration, 2010.

station of the Great Northern Railway next door at King's Cross. After years of being obliged to pay high access rates to the GNR for running its trains through to London, the MR could physically dominate its neighbour and rival.

It has sometimes been suggested that Scott's design for the Midland Grand was simply a rehash of his rejected Gothic design of 1856 for the Foreign Office, but they have only a loose stylistic similarity. Although Scott worked independently of Barlow, the engineer's site plan had already been accepted when Scott started work and he had to follow key elements of Barlow's layout, such as the entrance and exit routes and high platform level with ramp access from the Euston Road. Scott's neo-Gothic style for the hotel is clearly influenced by the great medieval cloth halls of Flanders, such as Ypres, but it is a very modern medievalism that incorporates obvious cast-iron beams and girders rather being a mock re-creation of the past.

The Midland Grand is undeniably extravagant inside and out, although economies were imposed almost as soon as the main building programme began during the economic downturn of the late 1860s. Scott took out a whole floor from his original design and work was carried out in stages. Construction started in 1868 and after five years only part of the hotel was opened to guests. The west wing was not completed until 1876.

High-quality materials were used throughout and costs were high. The Midland Grand was nine times more expensive than the Great Western Hotel at Paddington and more than fourteen times the cost of the Great Northern Hotel next door at King's Cross. Scott had no regrets, even recording in 1870 that 'it is often spoken of to me as the finest building in London; my own belief is that it is possibly *too good* for its purpose.' It had all the latest features of the time, such as gasoliers, electric bells and hydraulic lifts, although by the early twentieth century the hotel was felt to lack such essential modern comforts as central heating and an adequate number of bathrooms.

Barlow's generous station layout meant there was never any need to expand St Pancras beyond his trainshed. In 1902 there were 150 trains in and out daily, which could easily be accommodated. The *Railway Magazine* commented: 'At no time of day can St Pancras be called a busy station in the sense in which the word is understood at Waterloo or Liverpool Street. The long distance expresses leave at stated – and stately – intervals, the only approach to bustle being at midnight, when three important trains leave within five minutes of each other.'

In 1923 the Midland became part of the London Midland & Scottish Railway (LMS), which concentrated on Euston as its principal London terminus for main line services to the north, despite its drawbacks and illogical layout. The LMS did little to bring either station into the twentieth century but it did close the Midland Grand in 1935 and turn the hotel into rather unsuitable office accommodation. This was the start of a long, slow decline for St Pancras, with periodic attempts to close the station completely. Writing in 1949, just after nationalisation, John Betjeman saw little hope for it: 'I have no doubt that British Railways will do away with St Pancras altogether. It is too beautiful and romantic to survive. It is not of this age.'

Even after the furore surrounding its destruction of Euston, British Railways (BR) continued to consider proposals to demolish the Midland Grand and convert the trainshed to some other use. In 1967 St Pancras was added to the national list of protected historic buildings at Grade 1, but still no solution was found that might preserve it in a realistic and sustainable manner.

Eventually, an exciting and appropriate long-term use for St Pancras was found as the London terminus for High Speed One (HS1), a new railway between the capital and the Channel Tunnel. When the rail tunnel to the Continent first opened in 1994, Eurostar trains ran on existing lines through Kent to new terminal platforms at Waterloo. Trains could run at top speed only over the dedicated high-speed lines on the French side of the Channel Tunnel. Work on the first section of HS1 began in 1998 with the construction of separate high-speed tracks from the tunnel through Kent, mostly alongside the existing main line. Towards the London end, the HS1 route diverges to run through new tunnels under the Thames into Essex and below east and north London, emerging just north of King's Cross to curve into St Pancras. Physical work on this section began in 2001, with completion scheduled for 2007.

Creation of the new St Pancras International terminus was managed by London & Continental Railways (L&CR) as an £800m public/private partnership. Foster & Partners were master planners for the scheme, and chief architect for L&CR was Alastair Lansley, who had been project architect on the redevelopment of Liverpool Street in the 1980s. The challenge was to integrate one of the masterpieces of Victorian engineering and architecture with the operational requirements of a new, high-speed twenty-first-century railway.

To accommodate Eurostar trains as well as domestic services, it was necessary to double the length of the platform area at St Pancras. Foster & Partners have designed a low but almost transparent glass and steel box structure that extends from the end of Barlow's restored roof but does not detract from the dramatic interior view of the historic trainshed. The extension covers as large an area as the original station, but this is obvious only in aerial photographs.

Eurostar trains under the restored roof at St Pancras International, 2010.

The station undercroft at street level, once used for the Burton beer trade but never seen by the public, has been converted into a passenger concourse and lounge for Eurostar travellers, linked to the platforms above by lift and travolator. On the west side it has been opened up by slicing through the elevated train table to create a shopping and travel centre that feels like a pedestrianised street.

The great trainshed high above has been meticulously renovated, cleaned, painted and reglazed to give the station interior a lightness it never possessed in the grimy days of steam. A lifesize bronze figure of Sir John Betjeman, the Poet Laureate, who died in 1984, stands clutching his hat and gazing up at the roof. Betjeman would have been amazed and delighted with the transformation. If he turned to look the other way, he might have been less appreciative of Paul Day's huge commissioned sculpture 'The Meeting Place', featuring two giant lovers embracing under the station clock.

Betjeman would certainly have enjoyed the final outcome of the quirky tale of the clock itself. Removing the original, 16 feet 11 inches in diameter, to sell it to an American collector, was one of BR's less glorious acts of asset-stripping in the 1970s. The deal ended when removal contractors accidentally dropped and smashed it. A glass-reinforced plastic copy was put up at St Pancras in 1975. The original clock was bought by signalman Roland Hoggard, who meticulously reassembled the damaged pieces for display in his garden in Leicestershire. Its lucky survival enabled Dent & Company, makers of the original Victorian clock, to create a very precise high-quality working replica for St Pancras International.

The statue by Mark Jennings of Sir John Betjeman, champion of London's historic stations, at St Pancras International, 2010.

Scott's Midland Grand has also been restored to its original function as a hotel, but on a smaller scale, and with part of the building turned into luxury private apartments. This has been a separate project from the station conversion, but the two dovetail together visually, just as Barlow's and Scott's respective designs did in the 1860s.

St Pancras International was opened by Queen Elizabeth II in November 2007. Two years after the start of faster Eurostar services to Paris and Brussels, new high-speed Javelin domestic services were launched on HS1 between St Pancras and Ashford. When the Olympic Games come to London in 2012, fast shuttle trains will make the journey from St Pancras to the new Stratford International station in seven minutes. St Pancras now takes pride of place as the international rail gateway to London.

St Pancras old and new. The clock-tower of the restored Midland Grand Hotel by George Gilbert Scott (left) and the entrance to St Pancras International by Foster Associates (right).

# KING'S CROSS

WHEN KING'S CROSS OPENED in 1852 it was the largest railway station in Britain, and much admired. Sceptical shareholders of the Great Northern Railway (GNR), who muttered about extravagance in their new terminus, were told by the company chairman that it was 'the cheapest building for what it contains, and will contain, that can be pointed out in London'. He was probably right. The total construction cost of £123,500 was far less than the combined bill for the Euston Arch and Great Hall alone.

King's Cross was designed by Lewis Cubitt, younger brother of master builder Thomas Cubitt, who had developed much of Belgravia and Bloomsbury in central London a few years earlier. Lewis was apparently not related to Joseph Cubitt, Chief Engineer of the GNR, who worked with his namesake on the station. King's Cross is straightforward, functional and economical, a complete contrast to the ostentatious showiness and impracticality of the Doric arch and Great Hall just down the road at Euston. Lewis Cubitt announced that what he wanted to achieve at King's Cross was 'fitness for purpose and the characteristic expression of that purpose'.

The GNR arrived in London in 1850, at first using a temporary station at Maiden Lane (now York Way), just north of the Regent's Canal on the site to be developed as a goods depot. While the tunnel taking the railway under the canal to the permanent passenger terminus was being built, the very basic facilities at Maiden Lane had to accommodate huge numbers of tourists visiting London from the North for the Great Exhibition in 1851. Even Queen Victoria

King's Cross station ready for opening, 1852.

and Prince Albert had to make do with Maiden Lane station when they set off for Scotland by GNR in August 1851.

The permanent King's Cross station was built on a 10-acre site formerly occupied by smallpox and fever hospitals. The Cubitts created a pair of long brick trainsheds for the arrival and departure platforms, separated by a strong arched wall. Each platform hall

The King's Cross clock tower, 2010.

originally had a full-length glazed wooden roof, later replaced with iron and glass. At the London end are two huge glazed arch windows, with a clock-tower in between as the only decorative feature. The turret clock inside, designed by Edward Dent, was displayed at the Great Exhibition in Hyde Park, where it won a medal, before being installed at the station.

Just to the west and originally separate from the station is the Great Northern Hotel, a rather plain Italianate addition, also by Lewis Cubitt, that was completed in 1854. Unlike the Great Western Hotel at Paddington, which was put up at the same time, the Great Northern looks like an afterthought and does not appear to be integrated with the main station site. The odd curved shape of the hotel follows the former line of Pancras Road, which for years emphasised its detachment. It is now being renovated and physically linked to the station for the first time by a giant semi-circular roof over a spacious new passenger concourse with a large new Underground ticket hall below it.

The simplicity of the original station layout at King's Cross was soon compromised by the rapid growth of traffic and the lack of space to expand. As well as being the terminus for the East Coast main line from Scotland and the North, King's Cross had fast-developing local passenger services by the 1860s. A sharply curved branch line down each side of the station connected with the Metropolitan Railway to Moorgate, and a junction at Farringdon took trains to Ludgate Hill and over the Thames. These lines under central London were used by both passenger and goods trains.

In north London, branch lines built off the Great Northern main line soon brought suburban services in from Edgware, High Barnet, Alexandra Palace and Enfield. All trains had to be squeezed through the bottleneck of the King's Cross tunnels. Daily departures from King's Cross grew from nineteen in 1855 to eighty-nine in 1873, most of them suburban trains. It was a complete reversal of the pattern at Euston, Paddington, or later St Pancras. Between 1867 and 1873 the number of GNR season-ticket holders more than doubled to over six thousand. By 1881 it was approaching fifteen thousand. Additional tunnels were added just outside King's Cross and extra platforms were installed, but the pressure on the station was not greatly eased until the 1930s, when extensions to the Piccadilly and Northern Line Tubes spread the suburban commuter traffic on to the Underground.

The GNR became part of the London & North Eastern Railway (LNER) in 1923. The LNER was not the largest of the 'Big Four' companies, but it soon demonstrated the best flair for publicity and promotion. Virtually nothing was done to improve services for the

LNER's many long-suffering suburban commuters, but the glamorous long-distance departures from King's Cross were always in the news.

In those days everybody knew that the 'Flying Scotsman', Britain's most famous train, left King's Cross at 10.00 every morning for its fast run to Edinburgh Waverley. In 1928 it became a non-stop express, always hauled by one of the LNER's powerful pacific locomotives designed by Nigel Gresley. A large crowd on the platforms watched the first non-stop 'Scotsman' leave King's Cross on 1 May 1928 behind engine number 4472, also named *Flying Scotsman*, and today one of the icons of the National Railway Museum's collection.

Press photographs of the latest LNER expresses always showed departures from King's Cross, particularly in the 1930s when Gresley unveiled his A4 class streamliners on the new 'Silver Jubilee' service to Newcastle. After the war, when British Railways (BR) introduced the non-stop 'Elizabethan' express on the King's Cross to Edinburgh

The first non-stop 'Flying Scotsman' leaving King's Cross for Edinburgh, 1 May 1928.

King's Cross in LNER days with the 'African village' in front of the station, *c.* 1930.

run in Coronation year, 1953, this A4-hauled service was promoted in a special British Transport Films documentary. Soon afterwards, King's Cross and its environs were the location for *The Ladykillers,* one of the best-loved Ealing comedies, with Alec Guinness, released in 1955.

The glamorous image of King's Cross as the great departure point for the North, in which it consistently outshone its rival Euston, has always been at odds with the reality of a rather cramped terminus with poor passenger facilities. The area on the Euston Road in front of the main line station, where a Tube entrance was built in 1906, has been a mess for years. In the 1930s the mixture of tacky, temporary structures on the forecourt, which included a full-size suburban show home put up by Laing's, was often referred to by railway staff as the 'African village'.

Diesel replaced steam at King's Cross in the early 1960s, but little was done to the fabric of the station building. A modern, single-storey travel centre was added as an extension to the station facade in 1974, though passengers were still expected to queue for main line departures in lines snaking round the tiny platform concourse.

*Going North, King's Cross Station, London, 1893*, by George Earl. Wealthy passengers can be seen heading for Scotland for the shooting season.

This did not feel like the grand gateway to Scotland and the North. King's Cross was seedy, unwelcoming and increasingly run-down. A terrible fire on the Piccadilly Line escalators below in November 1987, in which thirty-one people died, seemed to confirm the area's reputation for neglect. It was, however, a catalyst for change. The station even acquired new fame after its appearance in 1997 in the first of the Harry Potter books, where the departure point for the 'Hogwarts Express' is the invisible Platform 9¾. Author J. K. Rowling possibly chose her site in celebration of a long-standing myth about King's Cross that this is precisely where Boudicca, warrior queen of the Iceni, was buried after her final defeat by the Romans in AD 60. Needless to say, there is absolutely no historical or archaeological evidence for this.

A master plan was eventually prepared for the redevelopment of the whole area between and around King's Cross and St Pancras stations. This has involved detailed negotiation, consultation and partnerships between public authorities and private-sector developers, which took a long time to produce results. Two large and spacious new sub-surface booking halls for the Underground station were completed by 2009. Better facilities on the surface within and along the western side of the listed main line station buildings followed, together with the renovation of the Great Northern Hotel, which had originally been scheduled for demolition. London's most complex transport hub, where three surface and six Underground lines meet in what had become an increasingly chaotic mess, is at last looking properly planned.

Just to the north of King's Cross, beyond the canal, 67 acres of former railway land, which once contained extensive goods yards, canal wharves and a locomotive depot, now constitute the largest inner-city regeneration site in Europe. Planning permission for this scheme was granted in 2006 and 2008, but development work will continue until at least 2020. It is an imaginative mix of new commercial office schemes, private and social housing, the refurbishment of historic warehouses and the re-use of other structures such as coal-drops, gasholders and a water tower, some of which have been relocated on the site. There is an existing canalside nature reserve and a new centre for the London University of the Arts. The whole environment of King's Cross, which has been run-down and desolate for so long, is changing dramatically for the better, but with key features of its historic railway infrastructure put to new use instead of being swept away.

Impression of the new glazed concourse between the restored Great Northern Hotel (left) and the western side of the main line station, 2010.

# LIVERPOOL STREET

L IVERPOOL STREET today is far more remarkable than the vast majority of commuters passing through it every working day will ever realise. Those thousands of travellers rarely pause to look at the architecture, and no City worker under forty will remember the completely different atmosphere of the station before its radical reconstruction in the late 1980s. The 'black cathedral', as Sir John Betjeman used to call it, has gone, as well as the elevated Edwardian tearoom that was once his favourite place in London for elevenses.

Yet Liverpool Street is probably the most successful large-scale heritage redevelopment in the heart of the City. The best aspects of a historic environment have been retained and integrated with a huge new office scheme on three sides and partly above it. Much of the station now dates from the late twentieth century, but it is partly in late-Victorian style to complement the restored and reinstated original features. Extensive demolition has taken place, including the whole of Broad Street station next door, but this project has also been a triumph of building conservation. It is now almost impossible to distinguish genuinely old from new, yet the result does not feel like a pastiche.

Plans for the construction of Liverpool Street were drawn up by the Great Eastern Railway (GER) soon after the company's creation in 1862. The GER was formed by merging five existing companies, which between them controlled all the railways of East Anglia.

Opposite: Sunshine and shadow at Liverpool Street, 1951.

The largest component was the Eastern Counties Railway, which had opened a London terminus at Shoreditch in 1840. This station, known as Bishopsgate from 1846, was just east of the City of London and not very convenient for passengers travelling to the central financial district. The GER already ran some trains into Fenchurch Street, but this tiny terminus could not be expanded. Negotiation with the North London Railway (NLR) to share its new City terminus then under construction at Broad Street came to nothing.

To develop its City traffic and build up suburban services, the GER decided that an extension of its line to a large new terminus of its own just inside the City boundary at Liverpool Street, alongside the NLR's Broad Street, was the only way forward. Bringing the line less than a mile into the City took ten years to achieve and was an expensive and flawed project. The NLR line to Broad Street entered the City at high level on a viaduct, but the GER chose to build their terminus with the platforms below street level. This was mainly to provide a through connection with the Metropolitan Railway, which in the end was hardly used and was removed in 1907.

To bring the line down to this level at Liverpool Street, the extension had to be built up a steep bank to Bethnal Green, which gave the Great Eastern long-term operating difficulties. Lord Claud Hamilton, the GER's last chairman, acknowledged in 1923 that building Liverpool Street at low level had been a serious mistake, which 'has been a great inconvenience to the travelling public … every one of our heavily laden trains has to commence its journey at the bottom of an incline.' In steam days this was quite a problem, and it remained so until electrification in the 1960s. Modern passengers barely notice the climb past Bishopsgate.

The first trains to run into Liverpool Street, when it was only partially complete, were suburban services on the new lines from Enfield and Walthamstow in 1874. The rest of the station, consisting of ten platforms altogether, came into use a year later when the old Bishopsgate terminus was closed to passengers. This was converted into a goods depot and used until 1964, when the main building was destroyed in a fire. The large original brick-arched support structure built in 1840 survived for another forty years before being demolished for the creation of the East London Line extension link in 2004. This new railway opened in 2010 as part of the London Overground network, reusing much of the former Broad Street approach route through Hackney, which had closed in 1986.

When Liverpool Street station opened in 1874–5, it was laid out in an L shape, with short platforms for suburban trains on the western side and longer main line platforms to the east. The long leg ran south almost to Liverpool Street and in the angle between the two legs there was ramp access to both sides of the station from the street, which is at a higher level. Tucked into the L round the access ramps were the station buildings, an unexceptional French Gothic-style office block in stock brick which rose to three and four storeys and a clock-tower with a spire. This was designed by the GER's engineer, Edward Wilson.

The platforms were covered by a very long and tall wrought-iron and glass roof consisting of two aisles and two naves separated by a double line of support columns down the middle. The great transept over the suburban concourse and main line platforms gave the centre of the station a cathedral-like quality, later enhanced by an elaborate four-faced Gothic clock, which hung over the tracks. The impressive roof structure was also designed by Wilson, working closely with the manufacturers, the Fairbairn Engineering Company of Manchester.

Despite the size of its new City terminus, the GER needed more space to meet the growing demand for suburban services to north-east London. As early as 1884, the company chairman boasted to shareholders that the GER could fill a thousand trains daily in and out of Liverpool Street but that their ten-year-old station could handle only two-thirds that number. Another 6 acres of land, between the eastern edge of the station and Bishopsgate, was acquired, and work began in 1890. Four years later the East Side extension was opened, with eight platforms covered by a much plainer trainshed. It was designed by John Wilson, Edward's nephew, and W. N. Ashbee, the company's architect.

Meanwhile, the Great Eastern Hotel was completed alongside the Liverpool Street frontage in 1884, designed by Charles and

Postcard view of the main entrance to Liverpool Street, *c.* 1905. Only the buildings on the right survived the reconstruction in 1987–91.

C. E. Barry in a vaguely French Renaissance style. The hotel was extended and doubled in size along the Bishopsgate axis in 1899–1901 by Colonel Robert W. Edis, who had just completed the Great Central Hotel at Marylebone. The Great Eastern was the largest hotel in the City of London, and its opulent interior included the rococo Hamilton Hall, the Abercorn Rooms and two Masonic temples – one Grecian and the other Egyptian. Two of the tracks in the station ran under the hotel to a basement loading bay, and coal and food supplies were delivered at night by a special train, which also removed hotel refuse and ash from the locomotive coaling bays.

At the start of the twentieth century Liverpool Street was for a time the largest and busiest London terminus, with eighteen platforms and nearly 1,100 train movements every twenty-four hours. Although it offered long-distance express services to Norwich, Cambridge and the Continent via Harwich, Liverpool Street has always been primarily a terminus for City workers. The GER deliberately built up an intensive suburban service from all over north-east London, and this became its main customer base.

Providing some cheap workmen's fares was a condition of the Parliamentary authority to extend the line to Liverpool Street. This was in addition to the requirement to rehouse residents displaced by the railway's demolition work around Bishopsgate. New tenements for six hundred people were built nearby at the GER's expense, and low fares were supposed to enable other workers to move out and commute by train. It is unlikely that many of the GER's new suburban passengers had been displaced from the slums of Shoreditch, but the cheap trains were a big encouragement to the development of Tottenham, Edmonton and Walthamstow.

By 1912, when Liverpool Street got a Tube connection to the Central London Railway, the main terminus above was handling 200,000 passengers a day. After the First World War this rose by more than 10 per cent. There was no space to enlarge the station again, and electrification seemed the only option to increase capacity. New electric trains were enabling lines in south London to offer improved suburban services, but the Great Eastern could not afford the high cost of modernisation.

Instead, the company launched an intensive new steam suburban service in 1920 which doubled the number of rush-hour trains. At the height of the evening peak twenty-four sixteen-coach trains, each with 848 seats, ran in quick succession over one track between Liverpool Street and Bethnal Green. This was an amazing achievement with manual signalling and little steam tank engines. It was soon christened the 'Jazz Service' by an evening newspaper and was still known as this right up to eventual electrification in 1960.

Passenger numbers at Liverpool Street had peaked in the 1920s, allowing the GER's successor from 1923, the London & North Eastern Railway (LNER), to postpone the inevitable electrification until after nationalisation in 1948. By this time the Liverpool Street suburban services to Epping had been transferred to an extension of the London Underground's Central Line. The first electric trains into Liverpool Street itself were on the suburban service to Shenfield, inaugurated in 1949. During its twenty-five years of running Liverpool Street, the LNER did virtually nothing to improve or modernise the station.

The original western 1874 trainshed in 1920, with a 'Jazz Service' suburban train at Platform 4.

British Railways (BR) announced the electrification of all suburban services into Liverpool Street under its Modernisation Plan of 1955. The last steam suburban trains on the old GE lines ran in November 1960, and two years later all other steam workings were replaced by diesels. This was the end of two unique features of the steam age at this terminus. One was the distinctive panting sound of the Westinghouse air-brake pumps on the tank engines, which had made the intensive Jazz Service possible with steam locomotives. The other was the sight of the two Liverpool Street station pilots, one an N7 tank engine painted black and the other a smaller J69 in Great Eastern blue. Both were always kept immaculately clean and polished by the staff at Stratford, the vast engine sheds just up the line in east London, which serviced more steam locomotives than any other depot in the country. The 2012 Olympic Stadium now occupies part of the old Stratford depot site.

A plan to rebuild Liverpool Street completely was proposed by BR in 1975. This scheme involved closing and demolishing Broad Street next door and creating an enlarged twenty-two-platform combined station across both sites, but buried under a huge commercial office development. There was strong opposition to this from heritage bodies and when permission was eventually given in the early 1980s it was for a considerably altered plan that retained Liverpool Street's 1874 West Side train shed and the Great Eastern Hotel. Liverpool Street was not to disappear below ground like the rebuilt Birmingham New Street or Penn Station, New York.

Work on the final reconstruction scheme began in 1985 and took six years to complete. Instead of a straightforward demolition and functional rebuild, as had happened at Euston, Liverpool Street demanded a more thoughtful and subtle approach that could blend heritage features convincingly with high-tech modernity. The Broad Street site was completely redeveloped as the Broadgate Centre after the closure and demolition of the station in 1986. The 1894 eastern trainshed of Liverpool Street was also sacrificed for air-space development as part of a separate commercial office scheme on Bishopsgate. A partnership for the co-ordinated rebuilding of Liverpool Street station, involving developers, architects and engineers was led by BR's Director of Architecture and Design, Nick Derbyshire.

The result was an interesting new aesthetic, where the retained parts of the original station were adapted and partly extended with replica features. Four new brick towers in Victorian style, inspired by the design of the Great Eastern Hotel, were installed in pairs to mark the station entrances on Liverpool Street and Bishopsgate. Inside, the listed western trainshed was renovated, with the acanthus leaf decoration restored to the 1874 columns. The whole roof was extended southwards to the new concourse and can now be distinguished from the original trainshed only by the colour scheme: off-white for the replica columns, cream for the originals to the north.

A light, spacious and airy new concourse is surrounded by an elevated steel and glass walkway with shops and cafés. The two main station entrances are on this high level, with stairs and escalators down to the concourse, where a new booking office and a spacious

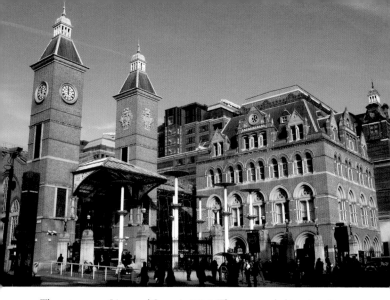

The entrance to Liverpool Street in 2010. The apparently historic twin towers (left) were in fact built in 1990.

The restored and extended western trainshed in 2007.

Underground entrance have been created. An unfortunate loss here was the Edwardian tearoom, which perched above the narrow stairs down to the Tube. On the high level to the west is a new bus station, and below it an arcade of shops leads out to Broad Street and the Broadgate Centre.

Everything has been transformed from the inconvenient and chaotic layout of the old station. Liverpool Street is almost unrecognisable, but all over the new station quirky architectural features and war memorials have been renovated, replicated and relocated. There was a deliberate attempt to recreate what architect Nick Derbyshire called the 'richness' of the old station, and these still make Liverpool Street an interesting environment to explore in a way that clinical Euston is not. The only way now to recapture the slightly sinister quality of old Liverpool Street, especially at night on the high-level walkways, is to watch the atmospheric black and white cinematography of David Lynch's film *The Elephant Man*, which was partly shot here in 1980.

The new station concourse in 2009, looking towards Bishopsgate, with the restored GER war memorial (middle right).

# FENCHURCH
# STREET

S MALL BUT BUSY Fenchurch Street was the first terminus within the City of London, and had the first station bookstall, operated by William Marshall, whose newspaper distribution company later came to rival W. H. Smith. A station was opened on the present site by the London & Blackwall Railway (L&BR) in 1841, just beyond the original terminus of its short 3½-mile line. Built largely on a brick-arched viaduct, the L&BR connected the Minories, on the edge of the City, with the East and West India Docks. The line was cable-hauled, powered by stationary steam engines at either end which moved a continuous cable, to which coaches were attached by a gripper mechanism, between the rails.

The L&BR opened on 6 July 1840, and a year later the service was extended to Fenchurch Street. There was no cable over the extension; incoming coaches from Blackwall were released from the rope at Minories station and continued up the short slope to Fenchurch Street under their own momentum. For the return, coaches were given a push by platform staff and attached to the cable at Minories. This was a far quicker way to get from the City to the London Docks than taking a paddle-steamer on the Thames, but the cable system proved unreliable. In 1849 cable traction was abandoned and the railway introduced conventional steam-hauled trains.

From 1850 a junction at Bow connected Fenchurch Street with a new line opened right across the north London suburbs through

Opposite: Aerial view, *c.* 1960, virtually unchanged since the 1850s. Air-space development and internal reconstruction took place in the 1980s.

Islington and Camden Town. Originally known by the lengthy title of the East & West India Docks & Birmingham Junction Railway, this company sensibly renamed itself the North London Railway (NLR) in 1850. The extra traffic brought by the NLR, and the prospect of more business from another proposed line to Tilbury and Southend, led the L&BR to enlarge and rebuild its Fenchurch Street terminus.

The new station was designed by the L&BR's engineer, George Berkeley, as a joint terminus with the London, Tilbury & Southend Railway (LTSR), which was part sponsored by the L&BR, and opened in 1854. There were five high-level platforms and a small passenger concourse covered by a single-arch all-over roof. The two-storey stock-brick station building at the City end has a plain but pleasant frontage on to Railway Place, topped with a curved pediment that matched the profile of the trainshed roof. Inside, on the ground floor, were two separate booking offices for the L&BR and the LTSR, with stairs up to the platforms.

Fenchurch Street station barely changed physically in more than a century, but had a complex history of operation by several different railway companies, at various times both partners and rivals. It was the City terminus for NLR services until the company opened a branch to its own new terminus at Broad Street in 1865. The first recorded railway murder took place on an NLR train from

An LTSR train arriving at Fenchurch Street from Southend, *c.* 1905.

Fenchurch Street in the previous year. Thomas Briggs, chief clerk of a City bank, was attacked, robbed and thrown from a first-class compartment of the 9.50 p.m. train between Bow and Hackney Wick on 9 July 1864. A young German, Franz Muller, was arrested, tried and executed for Briggs's murder less than six months later, on 14 November. This notorious and well-publicised crime did not appear to dent the growing popularity of the NLR's services.

In 1866 the L&BR, which owned the station, was taken over by the Great Eastern Railway (GER). The GER already operated eleven daily LTSR services between Tilbury and Fenchurch Street, as well as its own suburban services to the City from its new Loughton branch. The LTSR became a fully independent company in 1862 but was eventually taken over by the Midland Railway in 1912. This led to a curious situation at the railway Grouping in 1923, when Fenchurch Street became the responsibility of the London & North Eastern Railway (LNER), as successors to the GER, but the main services from the station, run by the LTSR until 1912, were now operated by the London Midland & Scottish Railway (LMS), which had absorbed the Midland.

The LTSR traffic at Fenchurch Street boomed in the early 1900s. Season-ticket sales nearly doubled between 1902 and 1909 as City office workers took advantage of the cheap fares and fast trains to move out to the coast and commute from Westcliff and Southend. By the 1920s Fenchurch Street was handling three hundred trains a day, with most of the fifty thousand daily passengers packed into crowded commuter services in the rush hours. Plans to electrify the line and enlarge the station had been announced before the First World War, but neither of the private railway companies involved could afford to do this. Some limited improvements took place in the 1930s as passenger numbers rose to seventy thousand a day, but full electrification of the Southend line had to wait until 1962.

A plan by private developers to rebuild Fenchurch Street with an office block on top of the station was proposed in 1959 but turned down by the City Corporation. In the 1980s a more sophisticated air-space development scheme was agreed which gave British Railways (BR) sufficient income to modernise the station completely.

George Berkeley's façade, now listed, was preserved and renovated but the interior was gutted and the trainshed removed to make way for the office building above. This is a stepped pyramid structure set back from the station frontage so that it does not overpower the Victorian façade visually. Escalators were installed from the old booking hall, now occupied by retail units, up to an enlarged concourse with a new ticket office and more shops. The design of the station interior is bland but functional and makes better use of the limited space available.

Fenchurch Street remains a curious anomaly among London's terminals. It is still the smallest of them all, and the least known because of its back-street location and lack of Underground interchange. It is almost exclusively used by City commuters from south Essex on weekdays and is deserted at weekends, but passenger throughput is over 15 million a year, while Marylebone is still below 10 million despite its resurgence. Forty years ago the future of Fenchurch Street looked uncertain but the oldest City terminus looks set to be busier than ever in the twenty-first century.

The preserved Victorian façade of Fenchurch Street, hemmed in by modern office development on all sides, 2010.

# LONDON BRIDGE

L ONDON BRIDGE station is on the site of the first passenger railway terminus in London, opened on 14 December 1836 by the Lord Mayor. The London & Greenwich Railway (L&GR), which built it, was a pioneer in bringing the first steam railway to the capital, but its ambitions were modest. The railway as originally proposed in 1832 was to be just 3½ miles long, running between Greenwich and Tooley Street, close to the southern end of London Bridge. The promoters adopted a scheme designed by a retired Royal Engineer, Lieutenant Colonel G. T. Landmann, who suggested that the line should be on a brick-arched viaduct. Much of the route was then still open country, mainly used for market gardening, and at high level the line could easily bridge roads at the built-up London end, as well as the Surrey Canal. It was also intended that the railway arches would generate income by being rented out as stables, workshops or even, rather optimistically, as dwellings.

The centre section of the line was ready first and opened between Spa Road, Bermondsey, and Deptford on 8 February 1836. Technically, therefore, Spa Road was the first London terminus but the line was extended to Tooley Street only ten months later. At the other end, Greenwich was not reached until 1838. London Bridge beat Euston by seven months as the first rail gateway to the capital, but the station was, in Alan Jackson's words, 'a very Spartan affair'. There were just three tracks and two platforms on the stub end of the viaduct, reached by a ramp and steps from the street below. The only station building was a plain three-storey block on the south side of the viaduct, which contained the booking office and company offices.

Invitation to the opening of the first London Bridge station by the Lord Mayor of London, 14 December 1836.

Up on the viaduct itself there was no trainshed, roof or weather protection of any kind for passengers on the platforms. A design was prepared for a triumphal arch, but this was never built.

Nothing remains of the original terminus at London Bridge except for part of the viaduct structure, which can still be seen at the Tooley Street end of what was formerly Joiner Street and is now a pedestrian tunnel under the station. London Bridge started small but grew rapidly into a large, sprawling station complex divided up between different railway companies. The little L&GR did not have aspirations itself to develop into a main line company but saw the revenue potential in giving other railways access rights over its viaduct to London Bridge, where it owned enough land to develop a much larger terminus.

The first such company was the London & Croydon Railway (L&CR), which paid a toll to the L&GR to run into a separate terminus just north of the original station at London Bridge. The L&CR station opened in 1839 with a proper trainshed over the high-level platforms and a booking office down below in Joiner

Street. Two more companies, the London & Brighton Railway (L&BR) and the South Eastern Railway (SER), also wanted access to London Bridge. This meant widening the viaduct to provide more access tracks and building a new joint station on the site of the original L&GR terminus, with an 'Italian palazzo'-style frontage designed by Henry Roberts. But even before the joint station was opened in 1844 the L&GR had fallen out with its clients over the level of tolls they were charging. In an effort to break the Greenwich company's stranglehold on entry to London from the south-east, the SER built a short spur off the L&CR's approach line to a separate terminus at Bricklayers Arms on the Old Kent Road, which was also opened in 1844.

Bricklayers Arms, because of its inconvenient location, was not a viable competitor to London Bridge as a passenger terminus. The SER ran regular services there only until 1852, when it became a goods depot. By this time they had achieved their objective and forced the L&GR to reduce its tolls to London Bridge. Under a new lease the SER decided to build its own station on the north side of the London Bridge site in 1850. Meanwhile the Croydon and Brighton companies had merged in 1846 to create the London, Brighton & South Coast Railway (LBSCR).

When the SER physically divided the London Bridge site with a boundary wall, the LBSCR was left to develop its own station on the

The 'Italian palazzo'-style joint station at London Bridge designed by Henry Roberts, 1845. These buildings no longer exist.

The Brighton side of London Bridge with LBSCR trains, *c.* 1905.

south side. The machinations and fallouts between a number of competing Victorian railway companies were the cause of more than a century's chaos at London Bridge. Decisions taken in the 1850s and 1860s have blighted its layout to this day, and London Bridge remains the most difficult station in the capital to use.

London Bridge developed as two stations side by side, and with an exceptionally fast rate of passenger growth. Between 1850 and 1854 the numbers doubled from 5.5 million to more than 10 million passengers using the London Bridge terminals annually. Both railway companies were pushing for closer access to the City and the West End, which they achieved in the 1860s with extension lines over the river to Cannon Street, Charing Cross and Victoria. At London Bridge this required the transformation of the SER terminus into a through station, with the Charing Cross extension taking a tortuous path at high level round Southwark Cathedral before bridging the river. The LBSCR side of London Bridge remained a terminus but was rearranged with more and longer platforms.

To this day the most impressive thing about London Bridge is not the station but the approach, where by the beginning of the twentieth century the viaduct begun in the 1830s had been widened to accommodate eleven parallel tracks. All of these are still intensively used by commuter trains on a daily basis, the busiest approach to central London. Electric trains were first introduced at London Bridge by the LBSCR using an overhead power supply for their South London Line round to Victoria via Denmark Hill. In the 1920s the Southern Railway, which had taken over in 1923, began electrifying all the lines into London Bridge but using the third-rail power system.

The full electrification of the Brighton side and removal of the overhead wires in 1928 coincided with the first breach in the wall between the two London Bridge stations. A new footbridge across the divide made it easier for the growing number of commuters needing to change trains here but did not solve the complexity of mass passenger flow through the station at rush hour. By 1936 the combined stations were handling about 250,000 passengers a day, largely concentrated in the morning and evening peaks.

During the Second World War the station was badly damaged by bombing but only patched up afterwards. In the post-war period passenger numbers recovered and grew even more, but a complete reconstruction plan by British Railways (BR) in 1961, to

Rush-hour bus queues outside London Bridge station, 1957.

be funded by commercial office development above the station, was turned down. Instead there was partial and inadequate redevelopment and improvement from the late 1960s onwards. The remains of the bomb-damaged station buildings were demolished, and the old LBSCR trainshed of 1866 was given a new roof. Two separate tower blocks and a covered bus station sprouted in the frontage and concourse area, which was remodelled, but none of this formed part of an integrated master plan for the whole site.

A final twentieth-century development came with the construction of the Jubilee Line Extension (JLE) in the 1990s. The Northern Line (then the City & South London Railway) had been the first Tube to run under London Bridge in 1900, with an

Morning rush-hour arrivals under the listed Brighton trainshed, 2008.

Impression of the new London Bridge entrance concourse, with the 'Shard' office tower development rising above the station, 2010.

awkward link to the surface station. A century later the JLE arrived and was ingeniously threaded through the crowded sub-surface structures and services. The JLE project architects and engineers used the opportunity to open up and revitalise the cavernous brick catacombs supporting the main line station, using them as an attractive access route to the Underground booking hall and escalators. Joiner Street, formerly a grim brick tunnel running below the station, was closed to traffic, cleaned up and converted into an inviting subterranean environment, complete with shops and cafés in the arcade. This cleverly reworked complex, now far more than a quick commuter cut-through, was opened in 1999.

The long-overdue rationalisation of the main line station above did not begin for another ten years. London Bridge is at last being completely rebuilt by Network Rail as part of the controversial 'Shard' office tower development, which will rise above the station. The Victorian trainshed, as a listed building, will have to be carefully dismantled for potential re-erection elsewhere, and a completely new London Bridge station will eventually emerge after more than 150 years of piecemeal development.

# CANNON STREET
# AND BLACKFRIARS

ANNON STREET is the product of Victorian railway rivalry. The South Eastern Railway (SER), which had brought its trains from the Kent coast as far as London Bridge in 1844, was soon in competition with the London, Chatham & Dover Railway (LCDR), which developed an alternative route to the capital across north Kent in the 1850s. When the LCDR planned to get direct access to the City by crossing the Thames at Blackfriars with a line to Ludgate Hill, the SER secured its own route over the river to Cannon Street on a branch from its Charing Cross extension. A triangular high-level junction on the new viaduct just west of London Bridge created the first rail link between the City and the West End via the south bank.

The station, river bridge and viaducts were all designed by John Hawkshaw, the SER's consulting engineer. Work began in July 1863 and Cannon Street station was opened just over three years later on 1 September 1866. There was a frequent shuttle service round to Charing Cross, the quickest way to get from the City to the West End before the District Railway opened along the Embankment. In 1867 3.5 million passengers made this seven-minute local journey, nearly half the numbers using the new station in its first year of operation. Nearly all main line trains in and out of Charing Cross, including the SER's Continental boat-train expresses to Dover and Folkestone, called at Cannon Street, and both long distance and suburban traffic grew steadily.

Hawkshaw's station was built on a great brick-arched base structure at the northern end of the railway bridge over the Thames.

Massive arcaded walls down both sides originally supported a crescent-shaped iron and glass roof over the platforms, with tall twin towers at the river end. At the other end of the trainshed the City Terminus Hotel was built by a separate company to a design by E. M. Barry. It opened for business eight months after the station, in May 1867, and was later acquired by the SER. The hotel's public rooms became popular for banquets and business gatherings, including, bizarrely, the meeting in July 1920 at which the Communist Party of Great Britain was established.

Cannon Street was electrified by the Southern Railway in the late 1920s for suburban services, and rush-hour commuter traffic became the mainstay of the station. The boat-trains to Kent nearly all ran from Victoria by this time, but some steam-hauled express services left Cannon Street until the early 1960s. The terminus and hotel were badly damaged by wartime bombs, possibly attracting more direct hits than larger stations because the bridge and twin towers made it such a prominent target for bombers flying up the Thames. After being patched up after the war, the overall roof was taken down in 1958 and the hotel, which had become offices, was demolished in 1963.

Cannon Street station and rail bridge from the Thames when first completed, with St Paul's Cathedral beyond, 1866.

Impression of Cannon Place, a new office development being built on the site of the Cannon Street hotel and over part of the station, 2010. One of Hawkshaw's renovated station towers is on the far right.

The station then went through two long phases of rebuilding over the next thirty years. At the City end bland 1960s office blocks were built in place of the hotel and over the station concourse, which was remodelled and linked to a modernised Underground station below it. The office block on the hotel site and over the Underground was in turn replaced by another commercial development in 2010. The main line station platforms at Cannon Street were left open to the sky until the late 1980s, when an ingeniously designed office building

The remaining columns that supported the original LCDR bridge at Blackfriars from 1865 to 1985. The cranes are working on the extension of Blackfriars station platforms right across the 1886 bridge beyond, 2010.

One of the renovated cast-iron pylons from the 1886 Blackfriars rail bridge, which carries the LCDR coat of arms, 2010.

on a steel deck was inserted between the remains of the great walls that had supported the original roof. The smoke-blackened Victorian brickwork and towers were cleaned and now bookend the black and white prow of the new commercial offices, as if enclosing a liner being launched into the Thames. Inside is a modern commuter station, but from the river Cannon Street's impressive contribution to the City skyline has been artfully maintained.

The next rail crossing of the Thames is at Blackfriars, just up river beyond Southwark Bridge.

Blackfriars railway bridge and station from the river, with a Thameslink train above and Thames Clipper riverboat service below, 2004.

It was built by the SER's rival, the LCDR, in 1864. The original bridge was dismantled in 1985, leaving only the iron support piers and granite plinths. On the south side are a striking pair of giant cast-iron pylons decorated with the railway company's coat of arms. These are now listed structures and have been restored in full colour, best viewed from the southern end of the Blackfriars road bridge.

The LCDR opened a station called Blackfriars here on the south bank in June 1864, which was a temporary terminus for their new line until they could run services over the bridge from 21 December, the first trains into the City from south of the river. A station was opened at Ludgate Hill in 1865, and a few months later the line was opened to join up with the Metropolitan at Farringdon. This formed the only north-south rail route through central London, which was to be revived in 1990 as Thameslink after decades of use only by goods trains.

Soon after its completion in the 1860s the line was being heavily used by local passenger trains run by several railway companies vying for access to the City from north and south London. To relieve the pressure from these commuter trains on their small through station at Ludgate Hill, the LCDR built a spur to a new terminus at

Holborn Viaduct, opened in 1874. This was then used by their main line trains to the Kent coast, but later became yet another commuter terminus as part of the Southern Electric network in the 1920s. After sustaining major bomb damage in the Blitz, Holborn Viaduct was reconstructed in a similar style to Cannon Street in the 1960s. It was closed in 1990, replaced by a new station at nearby Ludgate Hill named City Thameslink.

In the 1880s, the LCDR built a second railway bridge over the river at Blackfriars to another small combined terminus and through station on the north bank, opened in 1886. This was originally called St Paul's, but renamed Blackfriars in 1937. The original station building on Queen Victoria Street was a modest design, which was all the overstretched Chatham could afford, but showed the railway's aspirations in a list of fifty-four domestic and foreign destinations incised in the stonework of the façade. This included Bromley and Broadstairs, but also Baden Baden and Brindisi, the mundane and the romantic. John Betjeman once asked a booking-clerk here for a return to St Petersburg but was referred to Victoria Continental.

The LCDR was unable to survive as an independent company and in 1899 was forced into an effective merger with its more powerful long-term competitor, the SER. The new joint operation was known as the South Eastern & Chatham (SECR), becoming part of the Southern Railway in 1923. Blackfriars station survived the Blitz and was not modernised until the 1970s, when the street-level building was replaced by a new entrance hall shared with the Underground, and an expanded high-level concourse reached by escalators. Fortunately the destination stones were rescued and built into the new concourse.

Blackfriars now has a pivotal role in the development of Thameslink. Cross-London services through Blackfriars were first revived in 1990 and in the latest stage of this long-delayed project Blackfriars station is being rebuilt again with a stylish new entrance hall and the platforms extended right across the bridge. This will not only allow longer trains to use the station but includes a separate entrance and exit on the south bank, close to the original Blackfriars station of 1864, which closed to passengers in 1885.

# CHARING CROSS

CHARING CROSS is the only main line terminus conveniently serving the West End of London, being just a few minutes walk from Whitehall, Piccadilly and Covent Garden. It was a late arrival, opening in 1864 as a result of the South Eastern Railway's determination to compete with the rival London, Chatham & Dover Railway, which ran to Victoria, in offering a well-placed new station for its Continental boat-trains to the Kent coast. The SER already knew that more than half of its passengers arriving at London Bridge were heading for the West End. An extension

The Victoria Embankment at Charing Cross, 1867. The main line station (top left) opened in 1864. New main sewers and the District Railway are shown below a new roadway, all of which were completed by 1870.

further west across Southwark, bridging the river to a new terminus on the north bank, was essential. A new City branch off the extension to Cannon Street and a link with the LSWR terminus at Waterloo were both part of the SER's ambitious growth plan.

For its terminus site the SER acquired Hungerford Market, at the western end of the Strand, and for its river crossing took over the Charing Cross Suspension Bridge built by I. K. Brunel in 1845. The chains and ironwork of the bridge were sold and later used for the Clifton Suspension Bridge in Bristol. To carry trains over the Thames to Charing Cross, the SER's engineer, Sir John Hawkshaw, designed the exceptionally ugly Hungerford Bridge, which incorporated a replacement footbridge to Brunel's on its downstream side. One of the most successful of the Millennium projects in London was the addition of elegant new matching independent suspension footbridges on *both* sides of the rail bridge, dramatically improving the riverscape at this point by effectively hiding Hawkshaw's structure. These were formally opened and named in 2003, the Queen's Golden Jubilee Year.

Hawkshaw was also responsible for the design of Charing Cross station, which originally had a long, tall arched trainshed over the platforms. At the river end the approach over the bridge is elevated, with the Strand end of the station at ground level because of the steep rise from the river shore. The Embankment was built along the Thames in the late 1860s, incorporating both main drainage for London and the District Railway, which opened a separate station here in May 1870, just two months before the new road opened above it. This is now London Underground's Embankment station.

Across the Strand frontage, E. M. Barry designed the imposing French Renaissance-style Charing Cross Hotel, opened in 1865 and still in operation, with many of its sumptuous public rooms intact. Although some of the interiors survive, the top floors of the hotel were unfortunately replaced after wartime bombing by a drab neo-Georgian addition that is completely out of keeping with Barry's elaborate façade.

In the station forecourt stands an imaginative reconstruction, designed by Barry, of the memorial cross to Queen Eleanor that was erected in Whitehall soon after her death in 1290 by King Edward I, but destroyed by Puritans in 1647. The story of the building of the medieval Charing Cross is told pictorially in remarkable decorative murals, designed by David Gentleman in 1979, that run the full length of the Northern Line platforms below in Charing Cross Underground station. Barry's 1865 cross above was cleaned and renovated in 2010, giving it a new visual prominence that had been lost over the years.

In 1899 the SER and its great rival the LCDR combined to form the South Eastern & Chatham Railway (SECR) and began operating Charing Cross as a joint concern. In December 1905 the main part of the station roof collapsed suddenly during maintenance work, killing six people. The cause was found to be a structural weakness in one of the wrought-iron tie-rods, which had fractured. The SECR decided to replace Hawkshaw's roof completely with a new design. While this reconstruction took place and the station was closed, the Hampstead Tube was given permission to dig up the forecourt for the creation of a new Underground station below,

The Charing Cross station hotel and the memorial to Queen Eleanor, from the Strand, 1888.

Interior of the Charing Cross station trainshed in 1864. This is the original roof that collapsed in 1905.

which became the southern terminus of this new line when it opened in 1907. It was renamed the Northern Line in 1937.

During the First World War the SECR played an important strategic role as the British railway running closest to the Western Front. Many troop trains left Charing Cross for Dover and Folkestone, soldiers often travelled through the station when on leave, and ambulance trains returned here with growing numbers of casualties. In December 1918, a month after the Armistice, King George V welcomed President Woodrow Wilson of the United States at Charing Cross on his first post-war visit to Europe. Two years later the SECR decided to run all its boat-trains from Victoria, and the Continental facilities at Charing Cross were removed. The customs shed was demolished and all the foreign-language signs at Charing Cross were taken down.

Charing Cross became more important as a commuter station between the wars, when the Southern Railway (SR) electrified the suburban network inherited from the SECR. Little was done to the

Decorative detail on the Charing Cross station hotel façade, 2010.

station either by the SR or British Railways (BR), which took over in 1948, other than repairing bomb damage. Dramatic change came in the 1980s, when a huge air-space development project called Embankment Place was created both over and under the station. The office development cannot be seen from the Strand elevation, where the station façade is still formed by the hotel, but from the South Bank or Embankment Gardens the bulky post-modern office structure, designed by Terry Farrell & Partners, is now the dominant building along this part of the river.

Inside the station, the passenger concourse is still naturally top-lit through a glazed roof and has been fully refurbished, with the retention of the double-faced Victorian station clock above the booking office. Beyond the barriers the platforms are now almost entirely rafted over, with an oppressively low ceiling cutting out all natural light. The only historical reference in this rebuilt part of the station is the SR badging on the river front of the Farrell building, which is visible only from the outer end of the platforms. Charing Cross now looks its best from a distance, particularly when viewed over the river from the South Bank at night, when both Embankment Place and the Golden Jubilee footbridges are dramatically lit.

Right: Charing Cross double-faced Victorian station clock, 2010.

A night view of Charing Cross station (left) and the upriver Golden Jubilee footbridge alongside Hungerford railway bridge, from the South Bank, 2010.

# WATERLOO

**W**ATERLOO had a reputation in the Victorian period as London's most confusing station. First opened in 1848, it grew in a piecemeal and unplanned way until by the end of the nineteenth century some fifty thousand passengers were arriving at the sprawling station every working day. Today Waterloo is the busiest railway station in Great Britain, used by 88 million passengers in 2008/9.

In the Victorian period the experience of using Waterloo had almost become a standard music hall joke. The station's appearance in *Three Men in a Boat*, published in 1889, is a typical comic characterisation. Heading for Kingston upon Thames for a leisurely river trip, the heroes arrive at Waterloo by cab and 'asked where the eleven five started from. Of course nobody knew; nobody at Waterloo ever does know where a train is going to start from, or where a train when it does start is going to, or anything about it.' Eventually, they bribe an engine driver to make sure his train goes to Kingston. 'We learned afterwards that the train we had come by was really the Exeter mail, and that they had spent hours at Waterloo looking for it, and nobody knew what had become of it.'

This was an exaggeration of course, but the operation of Waterloo had become sufficiently chaotic for the London & South Western Railway (LSWR) to decide that complete reconstruction of their station was the only way forward. This took more than twenty years

Opposite: The 'Gateway to Health & Pleasure': an LSWR poster featuring the newly completed Victory Arch at Waterloo, 1922.

to achieve, but it created Britain's first and best laid-out twentieth-century terminus, the only one that could take both holiday traffic and a huge daily tide of commuters in its stride.

Waterloo was not the original terminus of the first main line from the South-west. The London & Southampton Railway, promoted in 1831, opened its route as far as Woking in 1838, reaching Southampton in 1840. The London terminus was at Nine Elms, just south of Vauxhall Bridge and close to a river pier that was convenient for goods transfer on to barges. It also gave passengers onward access to the City by steamboat, and there were horse bus connections with other parts of central London. But the railway company, renamed the LSWR in 1839, soon recognised the benefits of extending closer to central London, particularly when a new branch line from Richmond to Clapham Junction opened in 1844 and boosted passenger numbers. This line was later extended to Windsor and Reading.

The extension of just under 2 miles to the south end of Waterloo Bridge was built mainly on a brick viaduct to minimise property demolition along the route, but even so some seven hundred houses had to be knocked down, with the line snaking round Lambeth Palace and Vauxhall Gardens. Waterloo station was built well above

The Windsor line side of Waterloo under the 1885 roof, *c.* 1905. This part of the station was replaced by the Eurostar terminal in the 1990s.

street level at the end of the viaduct, with provision for further extension towards the City. No proper station buildings were erected in the early years, but the terminus grew, with extra platforms added in an almost haphazard fashion. On the west side what became known as the 'Windsor station', dealing with the Windsor lines and other local traffic, first opened in 1860, and more platforms were built on to the central station in 1878. A new roof was built over the Windsor station in 1885 and the approach tracks were widened in 1892.

On the eastern side of the approach, a separate private station was opened in 1854 by the London Necropolis Company, which ran a daily funeral train right into its cemetery beside the main line at Brookwood, near Woking. Brookwood quickly became the largest

Sir Winston Churchill's funeral train at Waterloo, 30 January 1965.

cemetery in the world but the one-way rail traffic from Waterloo did not become the main solution to Victorian London's growing burial problems as its promoters hoped. The Necropolis terminus was reconstructed in 1902, with a new entrance building at 121 Westminster Bridge Road. This still survives as offices, but the Necropolis station and funeral train service were closed down after taking a direct hit in an air raid on 16 April 1941.

The most famous funeral train to leave Waterloo departed from the main line station nearly a quarter of a century later and had no connection with the Necropolis Company. On 30 January 1965 a special train carried Sir Winston Churchill's coffin to Oxfordshire for burial in the churchyard at Bladon, near his birthplace at Blenheim Palace. This followed his state funeral service and procession through central London. The train left Waterloo behind the SR 'Battle of Britain' class steam locomotive which carried his name, and which is now preserved in the National Railway Museum's collection.

When the SER's London Bridge to Charing Cross extension opened in 1864, a rail link into Waterloo was opened, and five years later the SER opened their own Waterloo East station. But for many years the LSWR and SER could not agree on through booking arrangements, and passenger transfer from Waterloo to the SER's City terminus at Cannon Street remained difficult. Eventually the LSWR got its own access to the City when it sponsored a short Tube line direct to the Bank, which opened in 1898. The Waterloo & City Line, popularly known as 'the Drain', is physically separate from the rest of the Tube system and was run by the main line railway until 1994, when it was transferred to London Underground. A separately promoted underground railway, the Bakerloo Tube, running south to Elephant & Castle and north under the West End to Baker Street, opened a station at Waterloo in 1906.

The radical reconstruction of the main line terminus was planned by the LSWR's new Chief Engineer, J. W. Jacomb Hood, who was appointed in 1901. He designed the new station after a study visit to look at the latest railway terminals in the United States. Jacomb Hood proposed a large station with twenty-three platforms and a wide passenger concourse, all on a new superstructure, with a steel-framed frontage block housing the main facilities such as the booking hall, cloakrooms and refreshment rooms. The *Railway Magazine* was particularly taken with the large underground men's toilet hall, described in its December 1910 issue as 'perhaps the finest in England', featuring a marble floor, tiled walls, bathrooms and a hairdressing salon.

There were some economies, such as retaining the old Windsor station roof. This meant losing two of the proposed platforms, but the rest of the station was built to Jacomb Hood's designs, with a new nine-span steel and glass roof at right angles to the tracks over Platforms 1 to 15. Jacomb Hood died in 1914 before the station was complete, and his successor, A. W. Szlumper, finished the job.

The new Waterloo, with station reconstruction half completed, 1912. Part of the old station remains on the far right.

Electrification of the LSWR's suburban lines on the third-rail system started during the First World War, with the first electric trains running from Waterloo to Wimbledon via East Putney in 1915.

The decorative architectural features of the main frontage block at Waterloo, which contrasted with the plain practical engineering of the new trainshed, were designed by J. R. Scott, who was to become chief architect of the Southern Railway. By the 1930s his style had evolved and simplified into a streamlined Moderne, best represented in the rebuilt SR suburban stations at Richmond, Wimbledon and, above all, Surbiton. Scott's very different early work at Waterloo culminated in the monumental Victory Arch, a baroque gateway at the London end of the concourse which incorporated the LSWR's war memorial to its 585 staff killed in the First World War. Its unveiling by Queen Mary in 1922 marked the completion of Waterloo's lengthy reconstruction programme.

Waterloo became the flagship station of the SR when it took over from the LSWR in 1923. By the 1930s all suburban services into Waterloo and the main line from Portsmouth had been electrified, but steam remained on long-distance services to the south coast and the West Country. When a day in the life of Waterloo was beautifully observed by John Schlesinger in his classic 1961 film *Terminus*, a visual documentary with music and sound but no spoken commentary, the station had barely changed since before the war. *Terminus* captured many everyday scenes that were to disappear from Waterloo by the end of the 1960s: an army of porters meeting the boat-trains from Southampton and Weymouth, the all-Pullman *Bournemouth Belle*, and main line steam locomotives running alongside the suburban electric trains. With appropriate timing, the final steam-hauled services departed in July 1967 just as the Kinks' London lament 'Waterloo Sunset', written by Ray Davies, reached the top of the pop charts.

There were major changes to the infrastructure of Waterloo in the last decade of the twentieth century. The two most important developments were the construction of the Jubilee Line Extension (JLE) underneath the main line station, and the creation of the first international terminal for Eurostar services from the Continent.

Both projects made extensive and ingenious use of the undercroft areas at street level to provide new passenger access routes down to the Tube and up to the new Eurostar platforms.

The JLE booking hall was inserted at the Waterloo Road entrance formerly used as a bus station, avoiding a major intervention in the main line station. New escalators run straight down to the Jubilee Line platforms below, with a flat travolator connection in a deep tube tunnel to the Bakerloo and Northern Line platforms, which run below the York Road side of the station. The JLE opened in 1999.

By this time Waterloo International had been operating for five years as the first London terminal for Eurostar services through the Channel Tunnel. The new station replaced the 1885 Windsor line platforms on the north-west side, the only part of Victorian Waterloo that had not been comprehensively rebuilt in the early twentieth century. Nicholas Grimshaw & Partners produced a spectacular design for the Eurostar station. It is a modern interpretation in steel and glass of the traditional Victorian trainshed, running down the side of the main Edwardian roof and then extending in a gentle curve to cover the sleek, double-length Eurostar trains. Below the platforms, but linked by angled travolators, are a check-in and departure lounge and a separate arrivals hall.

This brilliant piece of architectural engineering was delivered on schedule in 1993 but not opened until 1994, when the delayed Channel Tunnel project was finally completed. Sadly, Waterloo International then had a working life of just thirteen years. Eurostar services to Waterloo approached London on existing tracks used by other trains and could not travel at top speed. When Britain's first high-speed main line (HS1) was built across Kent from 1998, a route under the Thames and across east London to St Pancras was chosen. When high-speed Eurostar services to St Pancras started in November 2007, Waterloo International became redundant. It may eventually be adapted for use by domestic services, but conversion will be expensive and it is not a priority, so London's newest rail terminal has been mothballed indefinitely.

# VICTORIA

VICTORIA was built originally as two separate stations alongside each other, later combined uncomfortably into one. Today Victoria is the second busiest London terminal, after Waterloo, but still split down the middle and showing signs of the divided original layout. John Betjeman described it as 'London's most conspicuous monument to commercial rivalry'.

None of the early terminals for main lines from the south was conveniently located for the City or Westminster. London Bridge, Bricklayers Arms and Waterloo were all south of the Thames, and the rival companies jostling for closer access to central London looked for an alternative way in to the west. A proposal by a new company to build a short connecting line over the river at Battersea to a new terminal site in Pimlico was approved in 1858. The Victoria Station & Pimlico Railway (VS&PR) was backed by the LBSCR and agreement was reached with the LCDR over use of the approach tracks and a long lease on the eastern side of the station site. The engineer for the VS&PR was John Fowler, who was already working on London's first underground railway, the Metropolitan. Fowler designed the Grosvenor Bridge, the first to take trains over the Thames in central London when the line to Victoria was opened in 1860.

Twin terminals were built on the station site in Pimlico. The LBSCR station, designed by its resident engineer, Robert Jacomb Hood, with a long overall roof, was completed first, opening on 1 October 1860. The slightly smaller LCDR terminus alongside, with an iron trainshed by John Fowler, was completed two years later. These two stations were run entirely separately and there was no physical connection between them, to the confusion of many travellers. Victoria's split personality is acknowledged in the well-known 'handbag' episode in Oscar Wilde's *The Importance of Being Earnest*, first performed in 1895. Jack tries to bolster his account of being found as a baby in the cloakroom at Victoria station with the added detail of its specific location on the Brighton side. This elicits Lady Bracknell's dismissive response: 'The *line* is immaterial, Mr Worthing.'

A third Victoria station was opened by the District Railway in 1868. The entrance to this separate underground station was on the other side of the cab yard to the north of the two overground terminals. There was no passenger link to the main line stations until a new sub-surface booking hall was constructed below the forecourt when the Victoria Line Tube was built a century later.

Neither the Brighton nor the Chatham company bothered to add any architectural embellishment to the joint frontage at the end of their original trainsheds at Victoria. Wooden buildings and boarding gave both station entrances a shabby, temporary appearance which was virtually unchanged for the next forty years. The LCDR's modest permanent buildings were round the corner in Hudson's Place, unseen then and now by most passengers arriving at or leaving

The arrival of a workmen's train at Victoria, 1865.

The Chatham side at Victoria, with a fleet of hired coaches waiting to collect the French rugby team and their supporters from a special boat-train, 1932. The 1862 trainshed by John Fowler survives today.

the station. The LBSCR's entrance was no better, but at the northern end of its station, alongside Buckingham Palace Road, an imposing grand hotel was opened in 1861. The massive three-hundred-room Grosvenor, designed in Renaissance style by J. T. Knowles, was independent of the railway company but gave Victoria its only real architectural presence in the nineteenth century. The impressive entrance hall, grand staircase and restaurant inside the hotel survive today, sensitively renovated and virtually unchanged.

The LBSCR eventually modernised its frontage in the early 1900s, buying the Grosvenor in 1899 and extending the hotel at right angles with a nine-storey building across the station entrance. The enlarged hotel, opened in 1907, was leased to Gordon Hotels for operation. The rather pompous new Edwardian baroque wing, which included much-improved passenger facilities on the concourse inside the station, was designed by the LBSCR's engineer, Charles Morgan. Many of the decorative details, which were later neglected and covered up in the course of the twentieth century, have been renovated. The station's best feature is a lovely tiled map of the LBSCR's network in about 1908, now revealed in one of the entrances from the forecourt. The map was obscured for many years behind a row of wooden public telephone booths, no longer needed in the age of the mobile phone.

At the other end, the Brighton station was extended towards the river and widened to the edge of Buckingham Palace Road to fit in more and longer platforms, covered by a new

The tiled LBSCR network map, c. 1907, uncovered at Victoria.

roof. This effectively doubled the size of the LBSCR station. The extension was complete by 1907 and was followed by improved train services two years later when the first stage of suburban electrification was introduced using the overhead wire system.

Not to be outdone, the Chatham (which had become the SECR) built an even more ostentatious frontage to its station next door at the same time. The building, designed by architect Arthur Blomfield, was lower than the Brighton's Grosvenor Hotel extension, but set forward from its neighbour and faced entirely in white Portland stone. Appropriately, as the entrance to the SECR's main Continental boat-train terminus, the wide central archway was set in a French Second Empire-style surround with maritime decoration including four statuesque mermaid caryatids supporting the roof pediments. The new passenger concourse inside the station was more restrained, but featured large separate restaurant and tearooms run by J. Lyons & Company. The old Chatham trainshed over the platforms was left untouched.

LBSCR 'Elevated Electric' train with overhead power pick-up at Victoria, *c.* 1920. This part of the station has been rafted over.

The SECR station was very heavily used during the First World War when it became the main London station for troops heading for France or coming home on leave. By 1918 thousands of men in uniform were passing through Victoria every day. Alan Jackson has described what became a regular scene at the cab arch, where 'almost every day, pathetic little groups of soldiers, families and girlfriends could be seen making their farewells. Relatives and friends were not allowed on the platforms for fear this might delay departures. Many, too many, of these men were never to see London again.'

The Southern Railway (SR) took over both Victoria terminals in 1923 and started what was to be a long process of integration by knocking holes through the dividing wall between the stations. The LBSCR's 'Elevated Electric' system was quickly abandoned and both stations were electrified on the London & South Western Railway's (LSWR) third-rail system, now branded by the SR as 'Southern Electric'. The rapid extension of the suburban electric network nearly doubled commuter traffic into Victoria, with wealthier season-ticket holders making a daily journey from Surrey, Kent or Sussex. Soon after the electrification of the main line to Brighton in

1933, the SR introduced Britain's first all-electric luxury Pullman train, the 'Brighton Belle'.

The SR found a growing market for its boat-train services from Victoria, not yet electrified but given the glamour and luxury of special Pullman coaches and Wagons-Lits sleeping-cars. The all-Pullman 'Golden Arrow' service to Dover was introduced in 1929, linking with a Channel crossing to Calais and its French equivalent, the '*Flèche d'Or*', taking passengers on to Paris. In 1936 the 'Night Ferry' was inaugurated, a luxury train of sleeping-cars which ran from Victoria to Dover, was loaded on to a special train-ferry to Dunkerque, and then ran through northern France to Paris Gare du Nord.

Imperial Airways opened its London headquarters and terminal building close to Victoria on Buckingham Palace Road in 1939. On 6 June the first SR Flying Boat train left Victoria for the Empire Air Base at Southampton. The Second World War broke out just three months later and most civil aviation was suspended, but some 'Air Specials' continued to run in wartime from Victoria to Bournemouth, linking up with Transatlantic Flying Boat services from Poole Harbour to the United States.

After the Second World War rail-air services developed with the opening of a new station at Gatwick Airport in 1958 and London's

The cab yard just before reconstruction of the station frontage, *c.* 1904. The Grosvenor Hotel is in the centre background.

first rail-air terminal at Victoria in 1962. A regular rail service to Gatwick for air passengers every fifteen minutes was eventually transformed into the non-stop Gatwick Express in 1984. The rise of this rail-air service was matched by the declining patronage of Victoria's Continental boat-trains. The last 'Golden Arrow' left for Dover in 1972 and the 'Night Ferry' service was withdrawn in 1980. Victoria's inviting international departure board, still topped with a sunburst clock and a pre-war header announcing 'THE GATEWAY TO THE CONTINENT', suddenly became irrelevant and redundant.

The ageing 'Brighton Belle' Pullmans were also taken out of service in 1972 and not replaced, much to the disgust of regular passengers such as Sir Laurence Olivier, who had led a customer revolt only a few months earlier when kippers were taken off the Belle's breakfast menu. Shortly before this, the main station clock, which hung over the Brighton concourse and had been the traditional meeting point at Victoria for decades, was removed and shipped to the United States to decorate a restaurant.

While some of Victoria's traditional features disappeared and its international atmosphere faded, the station became ever busier with commuters. It needed comprehensive reorganisation to a single, logical plan but commercial pressures and opportunities led British Rail to base the selective redevelopment of Victoria in the 1980s largely around exploitation of the air space over half the station. Most of the Brighton side was covered with a steel raft on which first an office block, Victoria Plaza, and then a shopping mall, Victoria Place, were built. The raft also accommodated a new rail-air terminal for Gatwick Express, but this side of the station now feels functional and soulless, its glitzy 1980s design already looking dated.

Meanwhile the main concourse and eastern side of the station, where the listed LCDR roof remains, has been partly opened up and the dividing wall replaced by a central retail block called Victoria Island. By the start of the twenty-first century Victoria was challenging Waterloo, with more than 200,000 passengers passing through every weekday. Further redevelopment of the station to make it fit for purpose seems inevitable, but after the partial rebuilding of the 1980s a comprehensive new scheme for Victoria is unlikely.

Victoria railway and bus station in 2009, a century after the façade was reconstructed. The Chatham frontage is on the far left.

# FURTHER READING

Bayley, Stephen. *Work: The Building of the Channel Tunnel Rail Link*. Merrell, 2007.

Betjeman, John. *London's Historic Railway Stations*. Capital Transport, new edition 2002.

Biddle, Gordon. *Britain's Historic Railway Buildings*. Oxford University Press, 2003.

Bradley, Simon. *St Pancras Station*. Profile Books, 2007.

Brindle, Steven. *Paddington Station, Its History and Architecture*. English Heritage, 2004.

Bryan, Tim. *Paddington, Great Western Gateway*. Silver Link Publishing, 1997.

Dendy Marshall, C. F. *A History of the Southern Railway*. Southern Railway, 1936.

Derbyshire, Nick. *Liverpool Street, A Station for the Twenty-first Century*. Granta Editions, 1991.

Hunter, Michael, and Thorne, Robert (editors). *Change at King's Cross*. Historical Publications, 1990.

Jackson, Alan A. *London's Termini*. David & Charles, 1969.

Jenkinson, David. *The London & Birmingham, A Railway of Consequence*. Capital Transport, 1988.

Lambert, Anthony J. *Marylebone Station Centenary*. Metro Publications, 1999.

Lansley, Alastair. *The Transformation of St Pancras Station*. Laurence King, 2008.

Meeks, Carroll L. V. *The Railroad Station*. Yale University Press, 1956.

Simmons, Jack. *St Pancras Station*. Historical Publications, revised edition 2003.

White, H. P. *A Regional History of the Railways of Great Britain: Volume 3, Greater London*. David & Charles, new edition 1971.

Alan Jackson's book is the only comprehensive history of all the London terminals but has not been updated to cover developments since 1969.

# Index